Daffodil, Snowdrop and Tulip Yearbook 2002-2003

*An annual for amateurs and specialists
growing and showing
daffodils, snowdrops and tulips*

in association with

The Royal Horticultural Society

LONDON

Published in 2002 by
The Royal Horticultural Society,
80 Vincent Square, London SW1P 2PE

All rights reserved. No part of this publication may be reproduced in any form or by any means, without permission from the Publisher

ISBN 1902896297
© The Royal Horticultural Society 2002

EDITORIAL COMMITTEE

M S Bradbury (*Honorary Editor*)

Mrs W M Akers

J L Akers

J W Blanchard

J Dalton

A J R Pearson

B S Duncan

Lady Skelmersdale

Opinions expressed by the authors are not necessarily those of the Royal Horticultural Society

Printed by Page Bros, Norfolk, United Kingdom

Contents

ILLUSTRATIONS	5
EDITORIAL	6
DAFFODILS, SNOWDROPS AND TULIPS *by James Akers*	7
THE HORTUS BULBORUM SHOWS THE GRAND HISTORY OF BULBS *by R. Degenaar de Jager*	8
A YEAR IN THE LIFE OF *NARCISSUS RUPICOLA* SUBSP. *WATIERI* *by Jim McGregor*	11
WORDSWORTH'S DAFFODILS *by Jan Dalton*	13
SPANISH RHAPSODY *by John Blanchard*	14
THE SEARCH FOR *N. LAGOI* *by Jan Dalton*	18
DIVISION 9 - A SYMPOSIUM	20
Overview *by Malcolm Bradbury*	20
Poeticus Ramblings *by Ron Scamp*	23
Sir Frank Harrison's Raisings *by Nial Watson*	24
Poeticus Hybrids in the USA *by Mary Lou Gripshover*	25
New Zealand Poets *by Max Hamilton*	26
Division 9 in Australia *by Richard Perrignon*	27
Narcissus poeticus in the garden *by Christine Skelmersdale*	27
CANADIAN TULIP FESTIVAL AND WORLD SUMMIT *by James Akers*	29
THE NOMENCLATURE OF SPECIES TULIPS *by John Page*	33
VINTAGE DOUBLES *by Sally Kington*	37
RHS SHOW DATES 2003	40
GROWING HEALTHIER DAFFODILS: THE BULB HANDLING PHASE *by Gordon Hanks*	43
MY WORK WITH THE GENUS *NARCISSUS* *by Frank B Galyon*	45
TRIPLOIDY IN *NARCISSUS*, THE FERTILITY DEBATE *by Peter Brandham*	50
AUSTRALIA SPEAKING WITH ONE VOICE *by Tony Davis*	54
THE FLORIADE *by Jan Pennings*	55
STARTING A SNOWDROP COLLECTION *by Matt Bishop*	57
RHS SHOW DATES 2003	60
YET ANOTHER *GALANTHUS ELWESII*? Notes on a snowdrop from Turkey *by Jörg Lebsa*	61
THE PETER BARR MEMORIAL CUP 2002: AWARDED TO MRS ELISE HAVENS *by Brian Duncan*	65

Daffodil, Snowdrop and Tulip Yearbook 2002-2003

OBITUARY
John Daniel du Plessis *by Ron Scamp* — 66

BOOK REVIEWS — 67
Snowdrops: A Monograph of Cultivated
Galanthus by Rod Leeds — 67
Tulip *by Richard Smales* — 67
Tulips *by Richard Smales* — 67

The Daffodil Society Cultural Guide
and Show Handbook
by Peter Ramsay — 68
New Zealand Daffodil Annual 2002
by Malcolm Bradbury — 70
ADS Illustrated Databank *by James Akers* — 70

DAFFODIL, TULIP AND
SNOWDROP NOTES
ADS Honours Sally Kington
by Malcolm Bradbury — 71
Are These Miniature Daffodils Extinct?
by Delia Bankhead — 71
A New Yellow Snowdrop *by Ruby Baker* — 72
The Cottage Garden Society
Snowdrop Group *by Daphne Chappell* — 72
Narcissus dubius as Breeding Material
by Peter Brandham — 73

OVERSEAS SHOWS AND REPORTS
Daffodil Shows in New Zealand — 74
ADS Convention *by Nial Watson* — 77

RHS EVENTS
Display of Miniature Species
and Hybrid *Narcissi by John Blanchard* — 78
Snowdrops at the RHS February Show
by Alan Leslie — 79

RHS Early Daffodil Competition
by John Goddard — 81
Results *by Peter Wilkins* — 83
RHS Daffodil Show *by Reg Nicholl* — 85
Results *by Peter Wilkins* — 88
RHS Tulip Competition
by Richard Smales — 93

OTHER UNITED KINGDOM SHOWS — 94
Daffodils and Tulips at the Harlow and
Kent Shows of the Alpine Garden Society
by Alan Edwards — 94
South East England Daffodil Group Show
by David Matthews — 96
The Daffodil Society Annual Show
by Jan Dalton — 97
Daffodils and Tulips at Harrogate
Spring Show *by Wendy Akers* — 100
Belfast Spring Flower Show
by James Smyth — 101
Wakefield and North of England
Tulip Society 167th Annual Show
by James Akers — 103

AWARDS
Wisley Daffodil Trials
by David Matthews — 105
Awards by RHS Committees — 106

DAFFODIL AND TULIP
COMMITTEE 2002 — 107

INDEX — 108

ADVERTISERS — 112

Illustrations

Front cover
Narcissus seedling 2108 'Clouds Rest' × 'June Lake'   (Photos Great Britain)

Page 36
Taxonomic presentation of the genus *Tulipa*

Page 38
A drawing by Mathias de l'Obel of a double trumpet daffodil from 1605

Between pages 64 and 65
Fig. 1 *Narcissus* 'Cantabile'
(Ron Scamp)
Fig. 2 *Narcissus* 'Vienna Woods'
(Richard and Elise Havens)
Fig. 3 *Narcissus* 'Chesterton'
(Brian S Duncan)
Fig. 4 *Narcissus* 'Killearnan'
(George Tarry)
Fig. 5 *Narcissus* 'Eastbrook Sunrise' Best Bloom and Best Unregistered Seedling (as G-001) at the RHS Early Daffodil Competition.
(Photos Great Britain)
Fig. 6 *Narcissus* 'Trimon'   (David Joyce)
Fig. 7 *Narcissus* 'Dandubar' Reserve Best Bloom and Best Miniature at the RHS Early Daffodil Competition.
(Photos Great Britain)
Fig. 8 *Narcissus* 'Jodi' Best Bloom division 11 and Best Unregistered Seedling (as 1736) at the RHS Daffodil Show
Fig. 9 *Narcissus* 'Whisky Mac'
(Photos Great Britain)
Fig. 10 *Narcissus* 'Littlefield'
(Photos Great Britain)
Fig. 11 *Tulipa sylvestris* subsp. *australis*
(Photos Great Britain)
Fig. 12 *Tulipa* 'Rory McEwen' flamed
(James L Akers)
Fig. 13 *Galanthus elwesii?* - green-tipped form
(Jörg Lebsa)

Fig. 14 *Galanthus elwesii?* - showing green markings on the inner tepals
(Jörg Lebsa)
Fig. 15 *Galanthus elwesii?* - growing near a rock
(Jörg Lebsa)
Fig. 16 *Galanthus* 'Tubby Merlin'
(Matt Bishop)
Fig. 17 *Galanthus* 'Viridapice'
(Matt Bishop)
Fig. 18 *Galanthus* 'Hill Pöe'
(Matt Bishop)
Fig. 19 *Galanthus* 'Greenish'
(Matt Bishop)
Fig. 20 *Narcissus dubius*
(John Blanchard)
Fig. 21 *Narcissus triandrus* subsp. *pallidulus* - with a split corona
(John Blanchard)
Fig. 22 A fine clump of *Narcissus cyclamineus* growing near Sigueiro
(John Blanchard)
Fig. 23 *Narcissus* × *montserratii*
(John Blanchard)
Fig. 24 *Narcissus* × *cazorlanus*
(John Blanchard)
Fig. 25 *Narcissus cyclamineus* growing beneath trees on the banks of the Rio Timbre
(Malcolm Bradbury)
Fig. 26 Elise Havens
(Louise Denny)
Fig. 27 Part of a display of tulips by Bloms Bulbs at the RHS Chelsea Show
Fig. 28 Jan Pennings de Bilt's display at the Floriade
(Joost Pennings)

Page 106
The RHS Daffodil and Tulip Committee 2002 (Photos Great Britain)

Back cover
Galanthus 'Ronald Mackenzie'
(Marie O'Hara)

5

Editorial

Regular readers of the *Yearbook* will have noticed that the front cover now carries the title Daffodils with Snowdrops and Tulips. This change of title reflects our decision both to retain daffodils as the primary focus of the *Yearbook* and to expand the coverage of snowdrops and tulips so as to appeal to a broader readership. We have been able to do this without reducing our coverage of daffodils by adding sixteen pages to this edition. Our ability to pursue this strategy in the future depends on both our continued success at obtaining interesting and authoritative articles and on the modest improvement in sales needed to make a real impact on the finances of this loss making RHS duty publication. As noted by James Akers on page 7 another important change in recent years has been has been the use of volunteers to provide camera-ready copy for the printers and thereby enable substantial cost savings to be achieved. This process has now been taken a step further by using volunteers to distribute the *Yearbook*, which will also continue to be available over the counter at RHS Enterprises outlets.

Our daffodil content this year includes coverage of two potentially controversial topics. In recent years, our annual focus on a particular division has highlighted the fertility problems, which constrain hybridizing activity to a greater extent in divisions 5, 6, 7 and 8 than in divisions 1 to 3. Two articles this year address this problem from different perspectives. Frank Galyon draws on his experience as a hybridizer and Peter Brandham clarifies and expands the genetic arguments he has deployed in several important contributions to the *Yearbook* in recent years. Both authors agree that it is sensible to include triploids in daffodil breeding programmes, agree with most of what the other author has said, but differ in their conclusions, in that Frank Galyon is more optimistic than Peter Brandham as to the fertility of triploids. An unexplored nuance in the current debate relates to the climate in which hybridizing occurs. Hybridizers in those parts of the USA, Australia and New Zealand where the Spring is either warmer than in the United Kingdom, or where the temperature can rise very quickly, seem to have had more success at breeding with triploids. Whilst in part this success may reflect a greater interest in the so called species based divisions and hence more hybridizing activity, another as yet unexplored issue is whether at the margin climate impinges specifically on the fertility of triploids and if so how. Secondly, our symposium on division 9 looks at the difficult issue of how to reconcile a wish to preserve a distinctive type of cultivar whilst giving hybridizers the scope to experiment.

Our Snowdrop content includes both help from Matt Bishop on which cultivars and species to include in a starter collection and a timely reminder from Jörg Lebsa that our understanding of *Galanthus* species is far from complete. Tulip enthusiasts will find much of interest in James Akers' report on his visit to the Canadian Tulip Festival and World Tulip Summit and in John Page's discussion of the nomenclature of species tulips and his plea for an up-to-date monograph on tulip species.

I am grateful to James and Wendy Akers for the many hours they have spent preparing camera-ready copy for the printers, particularly given the extra sixteen pages this year. I would also like to thank the many contributors of this year's varied articles and pictures.

Malcolm Bradbury

The Daffodil, Snowdrop and Tulip Yearbook

James Akers

The Royal Horticultural Society's Daffodil and Tulip Committee (DTC), formed in the last decade of the 19th century, waited almost 20 years before raising the idea of a daffodil publication. At their meeting on 14 March 1911 the RHS secretary Robert Sydenham reported that "he believed the council would grant any reasonable requests in connection with... a Year Book"

At the next meeting E A Bowles, the Rev G H Engleheart and J T Bennett-Poe were appointed to select the Publications Sub-Committee that, almost two years later on 18 March 1913, briefly outlined a proposed scheme for the *Daffodil Year Book* in which: -

All certificated daffodils be described.

The Daffodil Classification be included.

The London Show fully reported and varieties exhibited be listed.

Brief references to Provincial Daffodil Shows

Thus the publication was born and the first two issues of 1913 and 1914 produced; however it wasn't long before problems arose. At the DTC meeting on 2 March 1915 was mentioned "the possible non-appearance of the *Daffodil Year Book* in 1915" followed on 9 March 1915 with the reason - "large expenses incurred in publishing previous issues". Although the 1915 issue was published this was to be the last for many years.

The first revival

Once again, on 5 July 1932, the DTC decided to appoint a sub-committee to "take up the matter of the proposed *Daffodil Year Book*". The suggestion that tulips should be included in the publication was rejected. The reappearance in 1933 was awarded many column inches in *The Times* newspaper which began a report on Garden Daffodils with: -

"Among the lesser activities of the Royal Horticultural Society none is more important than the publication of Year Books, treating of certain *genera* of plants. That on lilies is in its second year, and now after a lapse of nearly 18 years, the daffodil Year Book makes a welcome reappearance... In the new book the historical aspect of daffodils has a place, and rightly, for much has happened since 1915; in fact, as a race of garden flowers daffodils have undergone a transformation. This has not been due, as with lilies, to the discovery of new species, but is solely the result of hybridizing daffodils among themselves."

There were eight issues before war brought an end to publication in 1940. A *Daffodil Year Book* 1942 was jointly produced by the American Horticultural Society and RHS but it is not included in the numbering sequence.

The second revival

Publication resumed in 1946 as *Daffodil and Tulip Year Book* until 1971 when financial losses again became a problem and publication was suspended for one year. To fill the gap the DTC "at no cost to the Society" produced the "*1971 Daffodil Season Report*". Official publication restarted in 1972 in softback form as "*Daffodils*" and later as "*Daffodils and Tulips*" without a gap in the year shown on the cover. The 1996-7 issue was the first to be produced using volunteers from the Editorial Committee to provide camera-ready copy for the printers, significantly reducing costs. A larger format book was produced the following year which continues to the present day.

The current issue sees two important changes. Firstly the inclusion of Snowdrop in the title to reflect the increased content regarding this genus; secondly the *Yearbook* will, as an experiment, be distributed by volunteers from the Committee. All societies who place bulk orders have been notified of the change. We look forward to an increased readership which we hope the new arrangement will provide. Please contact the Editor with any queries.

7

The Hortus Bulborum Shows the Grand History of Bulbs

R. Degenaar de Jager

In the early 1920s, Peter Boschman, the headmaster of the local primary school in the village of Akersloot, near Haarlem, observed that bulb-growers sooner or later stopped growing many varieties of tulips and daffodils. At that time some 5,000 cultivars were grown and listed. Boschman found out why a cultivar was discarded:
1. the variety had been surpassed by improvements.
2. the variety did not produce well enough.
3. there was no demand for the variety.
4. the planting stock was too small.

Peter Boschman realized that it would be tragic if perhaps important elements, characteristics, colours and habits were being thrown away. He did not come from a bulb-grower's family but nonetheless, he had the gut-feeling.

He had contacts with many bulb growers, was very interested in bulbs and could talk about them with passion and conviction. Peter asked his friend Nicolaas Blokker to help him collect the disappearing varieties of tulips and managed to save 150 varieties which he planted in his own garden near the school. Later when the collection had increased to 400 varieties they were planted at Vanhof & Blokker, who had been bulb-growers since 1868. They hosted the collection for 50 years.

Four years after the modest start in 1932, the activities were put together and legalized in a society by the name of Neversie. To everybody's surprise, the first open-days of the Hortus in 1933 attracted nearly 200 visitors. It was the success story of the bulb industry! The creation of the Neversie was an important step as it then received the recognition and attention it needed from bulb growers.

Today, over 150 horticultural writers, radio and TV journalists and reporters from all over the world visit the Hortus each year and report on the beauty and history of bulbs. It is a visit which is different from the Keukenhof as they are at the source and can touch the historic flowers.

Indeed, Boschman and his friends had no idea how valuable and important their collection would be for the bulb industry when they started their Hortus Bulborum project.

Conservation

The collecting and conserving the old varieties was the main reason for starting the Hortus. This still holds true and is considered a worthwhile cause. Growers like to donate discontinued cultivars, especially when they are from the raiser's family. The Hortus is now at the point where it needs to decide if recent introductions should be included in the collection.

The Collection

We have a considerable collection of various bulbs with 1,300 varieties of tulips and 200 old varieties of daffodils. We have recently added 750 daffodil cultivars from the well-known collection of Karel van de Veek, 60 varieties of crocus (oldest *Purpurea grandiflora* 1870) and 12 varieties of *Fritillaria imperialis* and *F. meleagris*.

All groups of tulips are well represented, included the Duc van Tols, the Breeders, Mendels, Triumphs and the old Cottage tulips. We have very few Bybloemen, Bizarres and Rembrandts.

The oldest tulips in the Hortus date back to 1594, and are the 'Duc van Tol' red and yellow. Then there are 'Zomerschoon' and 'Lac van Rijn' both of which were auctioned in Alkmaar on February 1637, only 16km (10 miles) from the Hortus.

Conservation and maintenance is costly and including the many recent varieties may not be in the interest of the Hortus collection. New bulbs are planted in our quarantine area to find out if they would bring in any virused or diseased bulbs. So we are careful in accepting donated bulbs.

We make sure that the different flowering times present the Hortus as a palette of colours during the six weeks that we are open for visitors. The daffodil collection draws much attention and is our early highlight.

Fewer cultivars

As all of us are aware growers and the trade have discarded a lot of varieties of tulips, daffodils and hyacinths during recent decades. To illustrate this I counted the cultivars of all bulbs in the de Jager's catalogues of 1948 and 2000 to compare the numbers 50 years apart:

	1948	2000
Tulips	400	140
Daffodils	210	140
Hyacinths	20	20
Crocus	50	40
Special bulbs	60	60
Total	740	400

This comparison illustrates the general trend. As everyone knows, it is mechanisation that enables growers in horticulture and agriculture to produce with a small staff and at low cost. Consequently, large planting-stocks are needed and there is little room for growing new exclusive varieties. If we are not careful all suppliers will end up growing and offering the same 100 varieties.

Gene bank

The Hortus collection also serves as a gene bank. Many hybridizers have used material from the Hortus and the results have been quite remarkable. IVT (a research institute forming part of the Agricultural University) in Wageningen have been quite successful in using our material; their results were good and useful varieties were raised, many of which are considerably less susceptible to disease.

Financing

The running costs of the Hortus are kept to a minimum and there are many volunteers to help out. Nevertheless, the total expenditure is quite high. Income is produced in six main ways: -
1. A considerable subsidy from industry
2. Sponsorship - mainly sponsoring a high cost item.
3. Adoption of a species or cultivar for five years.
4. Friends of the Hortus Bulborum - who have no voting power.
5. Income from visitors.
6. Sale of historic Hortus bulbs - for which purpose a special surplus of selected varieties is built up.

Some 5,500 people visit the Hortus in Spring, not bad considering that it is open for just six weeks. Of course, we advertise and do mailings to get visitors inside the gate. Visitors come from various countries and include garden clubs, service clubs, groups of senior citizens, tourists, students and schools etc. Every year, students from the International School in Brussels make it a point to visit the Hortus Bulborum and spend several hours listening, looking and comparing. Many bulb growers visit us frequently.

Guided tours can be arranged. We have a professional crew of retired bulb-salesmen who give expert information and language is not really a problem. It is fun to be one of the guides as the remarks and observations from outsiders are always interesting.

Documentation and Information

We work with the Laboratory of Lisse, with Wageningen and several bulb-growers. We are not active in preparing or publishing any kind of scientific documentation as we do not have the means, the expertise or help to do that.

We have the collection available, make researchers welcome, give them shelter on cold days and we feel that this is as far as we can go. For the same reason we do not have extensive information available. We are working on a complete planting list, giving the names, the hybridizer, and the year when the species or cultivar was first described or introduced. In the Hortus, signs give brief information about every group in two languages, which is well read by visitors.

We regret not being able to give more exact information. We find however, that the consumer is asking more questions every year such as:

Where and when the variety was introduced.

The social history or story of a particular variety.

If the variety can be naturalized, and increases well because "I do not like planting bulbs in Fall".

The questions indicate a growing interest in the individuality of varieties. The consumer wants to know and he or she is now spending lots of money with care - be it on perennials, daffodils, tulips or their wines.

The big threat facing the industry is outlets like Wal-Mart and that is why we must try to also grow and offer a wide selection of new, special, historic or old-fashioned species and cultivars and provide the information that the consumer wants to have.

Editors note [1]. This article is an extract from a talk prepared by the author and presented on his behalf by Jan Pennings to a meeting of the RHS Daffodil and Tulip Committee earlier this year.

Editors note [2]. Information about the 75th Anniversary and the Hortus Bulborum in general may be obtained from the secretary Mr Th Zandbergen,van den Endelaan 21, 2182ES Hillegom, Holland.

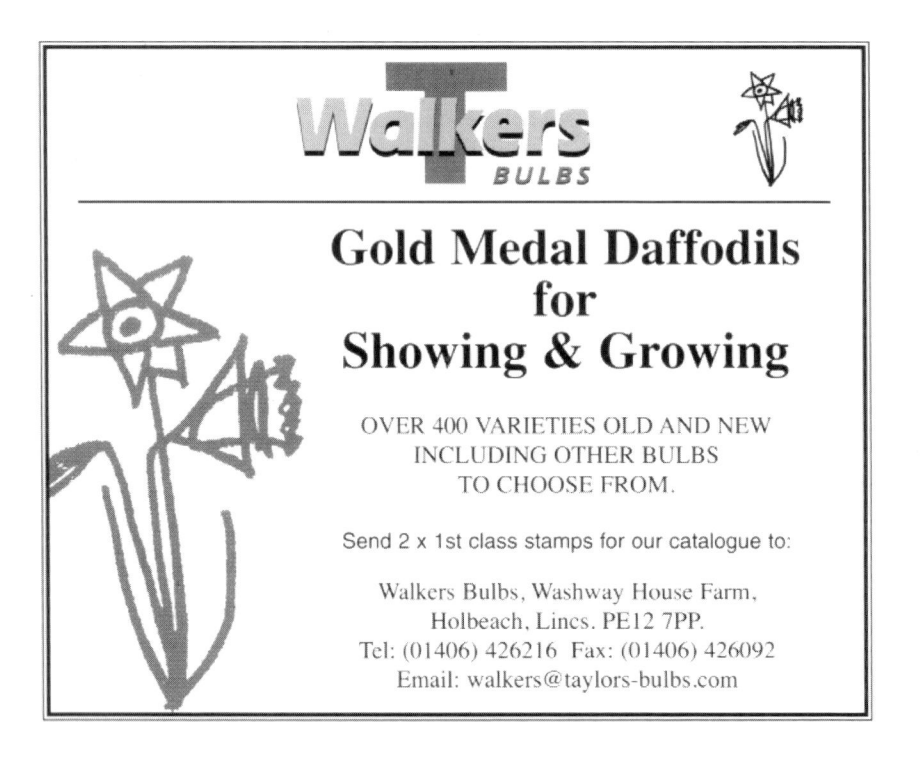

Walkers BULBS

Gold Medal Daffodils for Showing & Growing

OVER 400 VARIETIES OLD AND NEW
INCLUDING OTHER BULBS
TO CHOOSE FROM.

Send 2 x 1st class stamps for our catalogue to:

Walkers Bulbs, Washway House Farm,
Holbeach, Lincs. PE12 7PP.
Tel: (01406) 426216 Fax: (01406) 426092
Email: walkers@taylors-bulbs.com

A Year in the Life of N. rupicola subsp. watieri

Jim McGregor

Hailing from the Atlas Mountains in Morocco, this clear white form of its Spanish relative, *Narcissus rupicola*, makes fairly regular appearances on the show benches of the Alpine Garden Society. A photograph of one fine potful appeared in the last *Yearbook* (Fig. 3)[1]. Here we take up the story when the pot gets home and describe how is it treated to keep it in good condition until it appears at the following year's show. Similar treatment is applied successfully to many other dwarf[2] Narcissi.

April
All our dwarf bulbs are grown in clay pots kept plunged in gritty sand in a frame or bulb house. When a pot returns from a show, it is plunged once more and the sand is kept very moist while the bulbs are in growth. Foliage growth is still very strong at this stage. We have never found that allowing *N. rupicola* subsp. *watieri*, or indeed many other dwarf bulbous plants, to set seed detracts from their performance in subsequent years. The flowers are therefore never removed at this stage. Pots that are beginning to look crowded in flower are marked with coloured labels for repotting later in the season. We find feeding important for most dwarf bulbs, especially while there is visible growth, and at this stage, the pots are watered directly with tomato fertilizer every 7-10 days.

May
Continue to feed regularly as long as the foliage is green. Keep the plunge material moist. As the foliage starts to die back, cut down the liquid feed and ease off with the water to the plunge. Tie the seed stems and foliage in a loose bunch so that they do not get entangled with the seed and foliage in adjacent pots.

June
Watch the seedpods for ripeness - if you miss them, you will have a healthy population of seedlings in the sand plunge the following spring. As the pods turn brown, cut off the stems and place in a clean margarine tub to dry out for a day or so before extracting the seed. If you want to increase your own stock, now is the time to sow a little seed that will germinate in late winter and flower in three years or so. The seed is sown in a gritty compost, covered in grit, and left outside until germination, early the following year, when the seedlings are removed into a frame or bulb house for the same treatment as the parents. Any surplus seed is packeted, clearly labelled and stored in the fridge for the Alpine Garden Society seed exchange. By the end of this month, growth will have completely died back and the sand plunge should be drying out.

July
Compost and sand should be completely dry. Now is the time when Alpine Garden Society members who specialize in dwarf bulbs have the edge on growers of other alpines - they can go on holiday with an easy mind. Repotting can start towards the end of this month, although it is usually left until August and sometimes even until September. The pots and plunge should be kept dry until any repotting has taken place.

August
Repot if necessary. Show pots are usually repotted every two years and seedlings are left undisturbed for two years before potting on. The pot is tipped out on the bench, and the bulbs collected into another margarine tub before repotting in a mix of equal parts of John Innes No2[3] and sharp grit. The bulbs are planted about 5cm (2in) deep - most bulbs grown from seed will find their own preferred depth, so try and repot

at roughly the same depth as that at which they were found. The top 2.5-5cm (1-2in) of the pot are filled with sharp sieved grit. The pots are replunged and the sand is moistened slightly. Surplus bulbs can be given to friends or potted up singly for sale later at Alpine Garden Society Shows when in flower. If you have a light well-drained soil, they can be tried in the garden. I find they do not persist for more than a year or so in our soil and prefer to plant them in pots and tubs that can be kept dry in the summer.

September
The sand is watered thoroughly and a first liquid feed can be given directly into the pot towards the end of the month.

October - January
Keep the sand plunge moist and liquid feed once a month.

February
The foliage is in good growth now. Feed every 7-10 days. As buds appear at the end of the month, start turning the pots regularly, a quarter turn every few days, to maintain even growth.

March
Feed regularly and turn the pots every few days. If flowering stems show a tendency to fall apart, tie stems and foliage into a loose bunch and apply some additional water directly to the pot

April
Flowering time varies from year to year, but the pot is usually ready for another show in late March or early April. The pot is often sunk in a bigger pot in order to display the flowers to best effect. Water thoroughly, clean the pot or double pot as necessary, tie the foliage loosely together for travelling and pack carefully.

Editors notes
[1] *The author is too modest! This pot won the Farrar Medal at the AGS London Show. When subsequently the pot was emptied it contained 151 bulbs.*
[2] *Dwarf narcissi encompass species and cultivars which are of miniature (or a little larger) proportions.*
[3] *A compost made from sterilised loam, peat and sand in the proportions 7:3:2 and containing a composite base fertilizer.*

THE DAFFODIL SOCIETY
(Founded 1898)

THE SPECIALIST SOCIETY FOR ALL DAFFODIL ENTHUSIASTS

Providing companionship, shared knowledge and advice, and information on growing and showing technique for over 100 years. Please join us.

Details from the Secretary:
Mrs Jackie Petherbridge, The Meadows, Puxton, North Somerset BS24 6TF

Wordsworth's Daffodils

Jan Dalton

Earlier this year, I was invited by the National Trust to visit two of its properties in Cumbria and the Lake District National Park, to give advice on the long-term management of the daffodil plantings and wild daffodils on the shores of Ullswater.

The first of these properties was Acorn Bank Garden at Temple Sowerby, Nr Penrith, former home of Dorothy Una Ratcliffe, a well known author between the two world wars. She became known to her friends as "The lady of a million daffodils" because of her love of and extensive planting of daffodils in the gardens and surrounding estate at Acorn Bank. Later, in 1950, Dorothy bequeathed the house and gardens to the National Trust.

The second property visited was at Ullswater where the National Trust run and maintain much of the lakeside shoreline around Aira Force and Glencoyne Park and in particular, Wordsworth Point, where the vast majority of wild "Lent Lilies" (*N. pseudonarcissus* subsp. *pseudonarcissus*) made famous by Wordsworth's poem can be found. Here some 200 years since Wordsworth first transcribed the notes in his sister's diary, into what was to become one of the worlds best loved pieces of poetry "The daffodils", still survive; descendants of the original golden host. Inevitably since that time, there has been a decline in the total area now inhabited by the wild daffodils due to farming and tourism pressures. However survive they still do and even under all this pressure these little gems still manage to put on a beautiful spring display every year.

The main purpose of my visit was to advise on the possible influence and risk to the wild population from the close proximity planting of non-species daffodils (hybrids); in particular, one large planting of 'Carlton' immediately across the road from the lakeside wild daffodils. In addition there were a number of unofficial plantings by individual members of the public of other garden hybrids actually amongst the *pseudonarcissus*.

My visit was to coincide with the launching of "Ullswater 2002" festival of music and the anniversary of William and Dorothy Wordsworth's visit to Glencoyne Park in 1802. Members of the local press were present and recorded information on the visit and the daffodils. Many of you may have seen the knock-on effect as the National press and TV media all got in on the act within days of the visit. Fortunately my wife and I were in Northern Spain doing a bit of wild daffodil spotting when the "balloon went up" and we missed the rash of articles, radio interviews and TV presentations that followed our trip to Ullswater. Luckily all the media enquiries were dealt with by a number of daffodil enthusiasts and the exercise created the kind of publicity and public awareness that benefited everyone.

On our return from Spain we made a further visit to Ullswater in April when rather more daffodils were in flower than on our first visit. Further advice was given and the suggestion made that any "rogue" daffodils, not obviously of the wild *pseudonarcissus* persuasion should be removed to another National Trust property, leaving the wild population to do its own thing. Also the national Trust were taking steps to open up the site at Wordsworth Point by removing surplus non-native trees and creating less dense shade to encourage propagation of the wild daffodils.

These measures would be of long term benefit to the wild daffodil population and help to ensure that future generations of visitors would have the opportunity of seeing one of the few remaining major sites of wild "Lent Lilies" in the country.

For there is good news yet to hear and fine things to be seen
Before we go to Paradise by way of Kensal Green
G.K. Chesterton

Spanish Rhapsody

John Blanchard

Narcissus cyclamineus with its characteristic swept-back petals is a well-known plant in gardens and has been the parent or ancestor of all the hybrid cultivars in division 6. It makes a fine parent because of its early flowering and its durable and attractive flowers. But what of it in the wild? Although not botanically described until 1816, the earliest known illustration of it was published in 1608. Some time after that it became lost in cultivation for over two and a half centuries until it was re-discovered in Portugal in 1885 by Messrs. Tait and Schmitz. Tait then showed it to Peter Barr, who sent bulbs to his bulb firm in England from where it was widely distributed. The original sites near Oporto and elsewhere in northern Portugal and at Vigo in Spain have long since become victims of modern agriculture and forestry, and especially of urbanisation, and a myth has arisen that it can now be found only on private estates in Portugal. However, last year a chance chat on the internet between Brian Duncan and a Chilean correspondent Dr. Juan Andres Varras revealed that Juan had recently seen it growing in Galicia in north west Spain. He was able to give precise directions to a site at Sigueiro, so Brian, Malcolm Bradbury, my son Dan and I decided that we must go. Research indicated that late February would be the right time, so late on 19 February we arrived at Santiago de Compostella Airport. The next morning we set off for Sigueiro and within quarter of an hour we had seen our first flowers on a bank at the edge of woodland near the road. There were many more on the other side of the road, some in woodland and some in grass beside a stream at the edge of cultivated land. We then located Juan's site by the Rio Timbre just outside Sigueiro, and then found more further down the river. There was even a fine clump in a playground which was the old station yard of the Estacion Orosa Vilacide (see Figs 22 and 25).

Later in the day we drove round side roads to the east of the airport and found several more flourishing populations. We thought there was every reason to suspect that it is widespread in that part of Spain and this has since been confirmed by Jan and Lynne Dalton and others. Probably the only reason why it has been little seen in recent times is that few plant hunters go to western Galicia in February.

All the plants we saw were in excellent condition. Hardly any were over and few were damaged. There were still buds to come. Growth was vigorous in wet fertile soil. Stems were up to 22cm (9in) and the average probably well over 15cm (6in). Coronas were sometimes just shorter and sometimes just longer than the petals. Although most *narcissus* species are very variable in the wild we were struck by the uniformity of the flowers. There was hardly any variation of colour. The vast majority had untwisted petals. The coronas were rarely flanged or crenate and usually were slightly waisted. They were a beautiful and memorable sight.

N. tortifolius and *N. dubius*

From there we flew to the other end of Spain, landing at Alicante. I will not describe our travels in detail, because they were nearly all to places I have written of before and we found no species or hybrids that were new to me. I will only mention the highlights. It was a good year for flowering in most places, except Cazorla and El Almaden which were very dry. *N. tortifolius* around Sorbas was more plentiful than on my two previous visits. They were past their best, but first buds on some umbels were only just opening and there were buds still coming through the ground. A few stems carried as many as 15 flowers. The twisting of the leaves is an invariable characteristic, and most flowers had quite wide petals. *N. dubius* was more abundant than I have seen it before. Instead of re-visiting the site I know just south of Villena we explored a little rocky hill at the back of the nearby village of Santa Eulalia. This is quite small and of no great height. You could walk right round it in little more than half an hour. *N. dubius* grows all over it, not in profusion but plentifully. It seems to be tolerant of all aspects, sunny or shady. A feature which I had not noticed before is that the flowers are often pale primrose yellow when they open, fading to white after a day or two. This sometimes results in a stem carrying flowers of different colours. Stems with more than two or three flowers were unusual (see Fig. 20).

More species and a splendid hybrid

Having seen *N. tortifolius* and *N. dubius*, and a fine colony of *N. assoanus* at the foot of a mountain called Mont'go near Denia in the company of Derek Donnison-Morgan, Brian and Malcolm had to return home. Dan and I then set off for other parts. The trumpets we had seen last year in the Sierra de Alcaraz and Sierra de Segura were only just coming through the ground but we had a close look at some small yellow trumpets a few kilometres east of Alcaraz which Dan looked at last year when they had nearly finished flowering. All had only one flower on a stem and I don't think they were *N. alcaracensis*, their nearest neighbour. They looked more like *N. bujei* than *N. yepesii* or *N. seguriensis* (if indeed those so-called species can be separated). We saw little else of interest until we reached Santa Elena. Nearby on the road to La Aliseda is a colony of *N. triandrus pallidulus* which Brian and his friends saw last year and described as "golden". We found a small proportion of yellow ones among the usual paler colours, but nothing approaching the deep yellow of *N. triandrus concolor* which is found in Portugal. Nevertheless they were interestingly different.

We then spent a day around the Collado de los Jardines an area rich in daffodils and other plants. Of the narcissus species there are *N. fernandesii* below and *N. triandrus pallidulus*, *N. hedraeanthus* and *N. rupicola* above. The *N. hedraeanthus* vary from the typical species with short stems as little as 2-3cm (0.8-1.2in) emerging from the ground at 45 degrees or less, usually yellow with narrow coronas, to taller ones with stems of up to 10cm (4in) and flowers mostly white or cream and often with attractively petunioid coronas. I take these to be var. *luteolentus*. One cannot say where one ends and the other begins, as here there is everything in between. They all hybridize freely with *N. triandrus* to produce *N. × cazorlanus* (see Fig. 24) At it's best this is a pretty little flower sometimes with two in a stem and we saw lots of good ones. We did not get to *N. rupicola* until late in the day, but it was in full flower. It mostly inhabits crevices in large rocks, often with extraordinary clumps of rather narrow leaves and difficult to reach with the camera. Despite an extensive search, we could find no hybrids with either of the other species.

From La Carolina we made our way to Andujar via El Centenillo. Beyond that little town the road is unsurfaced for a long way, but passable. We saw little except *N. triandrus*, other than a small patch of *N. bulbocodium* with the inevitable hybrid. Then when we got into cattle country we saw some *N. jonquilla minor*. They were in a field occupied by bulls, so we did not investigate further! Near the end of the road at Los Vinas we saw some more beside a track, but the track was guarded by a large dog and the only local in sight was not helpful. Opposite, beside the road, was the most splendid hybrid I have ever seen in the wild, clearly *N. jonquilla minor × N. triandrus pallidulus* with five wide petalled flowers on a stout stem over 30cm (1ft) high. Even as grown at the Keukenhof N. 'Hawera' does not compare. We found two more specimens of the same cross near the southern end of the J5000 road. It did not have quite such good petals, but one of the stems was 38cm (15in) tall and carried seven flowers.

One of my favourite places in Spain is Los Rehoyos. You won't find it on the Michelin map but it is the pass on the road from Andujar to Puertollano via Mestanza where the road bypasses Solano del Pina. Just at the pass a track leads to a radio station only half a kilometre (550yds) away. Here one sees only two species, *N. cantabricus* and *N. triandrus pallidulus*, but both are there in great quantities. *N. triandrus* is as usual scattered everywhere, but the *N. cantabricus* are in great drifts. The hybrid between the two, *N.* × *susannae* (formerly known as *N.* × *munozii-garmandiae*) is to my mind the most beautiful of all the wild hybrid narcissi. This year they were more abundant than I have ever seen them before, both here and at the picnic site north of the Puerto de Mestanza. Although the triandrus parent varies in colour from pale yellow to white, almost all the hybrids were the same pure white as *N. cantabricus* with only a few milky white ones. They do vary in form, in the breadth of their petals, the degree to which the petals are reflexed and in the proportions of the corona, but mostly all are elegant and attractive. Some plants looked more vigorous than others. Yellow hybrids have been seen at this site on the other side of the road, but we could not find any.

A wild split-corona daffodil
We also saw two interesting variants of *N. triandrus* subsp. *pallidulus* here. One was a semi-double, the doubling only affecting three of the anthers but not the petals or the corona. The other was a genuine split-corona, with the corona divided into six segments right to the base and spread out wide (see Fig. 21). We saw more of these further on, south of the Collado de Pontonar. I found them curiously attractive.

A second visit to Spain
Having written thus far, I thought that my daffodil hunting for the year was over. But then I received an unexpected invitation to join Brian and Betty Duncan for eight days in northern Spain. We flew to Madrid on 7 May and spent the first day around Puerto de Navacerrada looking at *N. rupicola*, *N. bulbocodium graellsii* and *N. triandrus pallidulus*. Then we headed for the Pyrenees starting at Benasque. Above the village is the ski resort of Cerler, and above that a huge car park at the foot of two ski lifts. On a previous visit I had explored mainly to the east and south of the car park. This time we went to the western side and found *N. moschatus* with its white trumpets and drooping petals in far greater profusion than I had seen them before. *Flora Europaea* tells us that *N. alpestris* cannot be distinguished from *N. moschatus*, and the latter being the older name is the one that ought to be used. I would like to think that the smallest ones could still be called *N. moschatus* var. *alpestris*, but there is no way that a dividing line can be drawn. Stems varied in length from under 10cm (4in) to well over 20cm (8in), petals from under 20mm (0.8in) to over 35mm (1.4in) and coronas from 16mm (0.6in) to 39mm (1.6in). There were thousands of flowers, and one could probably find more extreme measurements than these and everything in between. The colour of the flowers also varied. A few were snow white. Most were off white or pale creamy white, but a significant number were pale creamy yellow. The colour of these match exactly the plant described from the eastern Pyrenees as *N. moleroi*. I adhere to my previously expressed opinion that this is a colour variant of *N. moschatus* and it is absurd to say that it is a separate species.

A day in France enveloped us in thick cloud at Superbagnères and rather spoilt the view of *N. bicolor*, but later the weather improved and we had a good afternoon in the valley up to Bourg-d'Oueil. Behind the Church at Ceres was the biggest field of *N. abscissus* I have seen, and there were large fields of *N. poeticus* not yet fully out and a few hybrids between the two.

Just below Arties in the Val d'Aran is a steep north facing hillside with many more *N. abscissus* including golden yellow ones and *N. poeti-*

cus sprinkled in among them. Not surprisingly there were many hybrids to which the name *N. montserratii* is given. Most were pale yellow rather like *N. abscissus* but with shorter coronas, but a few took some colour from the *N. poeticus* parent. Some were pale orange, but I found one rather exciting one with white petals and an almost pinkish orange medium length corona (see Fig. 23). Kathy Andersen found one with yellow petals and a deep orange corona.

We had a beautiful day in Andorra where *N. pallidiflorus* was flowering in profusion in the Val d'Incles. *N. poeticus* is also plentiful in that valley, but none were out and buds were only just coming through the ground. I know that there are hybrids there, but it seems that they all flower later.

Another foray into France took us over the 2,001m (6,600ft) Col du Pradel where snow was still lying at the side of the road. Both sides of the pass we saw *N. abscissus* again, but here instead of their usually cylindrical unflared trumpets, they had a neatly serrated little flange. I found them most attractive.

Finally, back in Spain, between Supermolina and Castellar de N'Hug we stopped at the Col de la Crueta and were rewarded by seeing above the road an extensive hillside with many trumpets in full flower. This is one of the sites, it may be the type locality, for the so-called *N. moleroi*. They were mostly concolourous very pale yellow, rather paler than *N. pallidiflorus*, but there were just a few which had slightly deeper coloured coronas.

On the two trips, having driven nearly 5,500km (3,440miles) and flown a few too, we found 23 species and 7 hybrids in flower. What a wonderful country.

The American Daffodil Society

founded in 1954, invites you to join with over 1400 members around the world to learn the latest cultural information, hints on improving showing technique, and in-depth reports on the newest daffodils. All members receive *The Daffodil Journal*, a 64-page quarterly publication.

Now available: The Illustrated Data Bank, which lists the life histories and descriptions of over 13,000 daffodils, including over 4000 photos. On CD-ROM in either IBM or Macintosh format. $150. Write for computer system requirements.

Memberships are accepted at the rate of $20·00 per year or $50·00 for three years (dollar checks or bank draft, please).

AMERICAN DAFFODIL SOCIETY, INC.
Naomi Liggett, Executive Director
4126 Winfield Rd, Columbus, OH 43220-4606

The Search for N. Lagoi

Jan Dalton

These notes come as a brief complement to the preceding detailed report of the trip made by Brian Duncan, Malcolm Bradbury, John and Dan Blanchard in February 2002, to the province of Galicia in north west Spain. The main purpose of that visit being to observe, confirm and record *N. cyclamineus* growing in the wild.

Fully a month after that trip, my wife Lynne and I made our annual pilgrimage to northern Spain in the hope of finding "something" different from the season we usually encounter in May, some two months ahead. Half expecting some colder and wetter weather than in May, we took plenty of warmer clothes and waterproofs in readiness. Needless to say, we ended up not needing them as we enjoyed ten of the most glorious days we have ever had in Spain as the northern half of the Iberian peninsula basked in an early heat wave.

Not having seen *N. cyclamineus* growing in the wild before, we too headed for Galicia and the general area visited by the earlier party. Our worry was the month difference and the very warm weather that prevailed during that time. Would they be over? Unbelievably, we found *N. cyclamineus* in their hundreds and apart from the early flowers which had gone over and were now setting seed we still found hundreds in peak condition and noted many other locations where this most beautiful of narcissus species were still growing in profusion. What a gem it is. I should add that we found it in several locations where it was flowering alongside *N. bulbocodium* but after careful inspection no hybrids or cross-fertilization was evident.

Absolutely delighted with our sightings we moved on to one of our other quests, which was to attempt to locate a daffodil species that John Blanchard had reliably informed me had not been seen or reported since 1909. This was *Narcissus lagoi* described by John in his book *Narcissus; A Guide to Wild Daffodils*, Alpine Garden Society 1990. Several years ago, Lynne and I had found a small trumpet daffodil in Galicia that was to all intents and purposes a larger version of *Narcissus asturiensis*, though quite obviously not *N. asturiensis* the type. On describing this flower to John in conversation earlier in the year, he suggested that what we had seen might possibly be *N. lagoi*.

Having got over the initial excitement of finding more *N. cyclamineus* than I believed even existed, we set off one evening into the foothills of the somewhat diminutive mountains of Galicia a few miles west of Lugo, diminutive, that is, by comparison with the Picos de Europa or the Pyrenees further east. After numerous sightings of *N. bulbocodium* we stopped at a small stream where in the corner there appeared to be more of the same. I wandered across to the bottom of the field that skirted the stream just to confirm what we had seen from the car with binoculars. Yes, they were the usual *N. bulbocodium* subsp. *bulbocodium* var. *bulbocodium* found throughout northern Spain. However along the banks of the stream on the other side I noticed some other daffodil foliage dotted here and there with fairly prominent seed pods. What could they be, more cyclamineus in this location? I thought not since the foliage was bluish green and larger than the *N. cyclamineus* we had seen so much of earlier in the day.

Having traversed the bridge and parked the car off the road I approached the stream from the other side and under the shade of the small bank side trees and shrubs I found more of the foliage and developing seedpods. Eventually I found what I hoped would be there, a couple of late blooming flowers still in quite reasonable condition. On closer examination the flowers were asturiensis-like in appearance, though slightly larger and the foliage was much broader, taller and bluer than *N. asturiensis*.

I dashed back to the car to get the camera and written description of *N. lagoi* in John's book, the expression on my face obviously giving the game away because Lynne said "you've found it haven't you"? I was hopeful that I had. The description in the book, though vague, seemed to fit the plant, the location was geographically close, so we agreed that it was very probably *N. lagoi* and what else could it be if it wasn't?

Had we been there a month earlier, we would have seen many more flowers and got a better "feel" for the plant and its peak season appearance. Early and late flowers can be slightly different in appearance, for one reason or another. The answer then is for an earlier visit next year in the hope of seeing more flowers. As John says, how many people visit Galicia in February to look for wild daffodils – which is probably why *N. lagoi* has remained unobserved or unreported for so long.

John also questions why it was given the name *N. lagoi* and not *N. lugoi*? It might well be that the original gathering in 1909 came from the vicinity of one or more local villages called Lago, that seem to crop up here and there, though not shown on all maps. This is only speculation on my part however.

We also made a day trip to northern Portugal and the Serra da Gerez where we found *N. pumilus*, though only a small quantity. On our return journey to the Picos de Europa we also found *N. asturiensis* by the million, all in peak condition, including a double version that looked like a miniature 'Van Sion'. If this were what you can expect to see in March, then we would gladly go again then. Of course, the good weather played a major part in our success and had the heat wave been snow things might have been totally different.

RA Scamp
Quality Daffodils

For a Colour Illustrated Catalogue of our Modern and Historical Daffodils.

Please send 3 first class stamps to:–
RA Scamp, 14 Roscarrack Close, Falmouth,
Cornwall TR11 4PJ
Tel/Fax: 01326 317959
Email: rascamp@daffodils.uk.com
Website: www.daffodils.uk.com

DIVISION 9
A SYMPOSIUM

"Anyone who takes to breeding should sow a few seeds of the poets, as an obeisance to a main founder species of the whole modern family, an insurance against the poets' complete submersion in the tide of modern breeding, and a very sure way of knowing that at least some of the seedlings are going to be quality flowers." [Michael Jefferson-Brown. (1991). *Narcissus*. Batsford, London.]

This year our symposium looks at the Poeticus daffodil cultivars in division 9. Statistically, division 9 is a small division, accounting for only 696 (2.7 per cent) of the 25,672 cultivar entries in the International Daffodil Register at the end of June 2001. Relative to other species based divisions, registrations of Poeticus cultivars are less numerous than Tazetta cultivars, but greater than those in each of divisions 5, 6, 7, and 10. However, as is often the case, statistics do not tell the whole story. Given their late relative flowering times, Poeticus cultivars extend the daffodil season, providing a final flourish, whether in the garden or at shows. Division 9 also provides a worrying classification dilemma; how do we enable hybridizers to experiment in division 9, without running the risk that the resulting cultivars will rapidly become indistinguishable from similar daffodils in division 3?

The symposium is in two parts, an overview by Malcolm Bradbury and a range of cultivar surveys by Ron Scamp, Nial Watson, Mary Lou Gripshover, Max Hamilton and Richard Perrignon. Christine Skelmersdale reviews those Poeticus species and cultivars that do well in the garden.

OVERVIEW
MALCOLM BRADBURY

This overview considers: -
  Show results in the United Kingdom.
  The evolving definition of division 9.
  What is "different" about how we define division 9?
  The consequences of our current approach to division 9.
  Where next?
  Breeding activity.
  Breeding needs and trends.

Though I am a member of the Narcissus Classification Advisory Committee of the Royal Horticultural Society, it should be clearly understood that the views expressed below are my own and not necessarily those of the Committee.

Show results in the United Kingdom
'Cantabile' 9W-GWY (see Fig. 1) was Reserve Best Bloom in show at the RHS Late Daffodil Competition in 1999 and also has a respectable record of Best Bloom in divisions 5-9 awards. Many exhibitors grow a few cultivars from division 9 and the relevant single bloom classes at major late shows in the United Kingdom are usually moderately well contested. However, probably because of concerns about size and balance, division 9 cultivars are seldom used in mixed collection classes. Division 9 cultivars have failed to feature in the top ten cultivars listed in the decade 1992-2002, in the "Summary of Prizewinning Flowers" published annually in the Daffodil Society's *Journal*. The same source also reveals that results have been dominated by 'Cantabile' which was raised by Guy Wilson before 1932 and which has more recently been

joined by 'Killearnan' 9W-GYR (see Fig. 4), a controversial cultivar raised by John Lea and registered by Clive Postles in 1985 and which is discussed in more detail below. Other cultivars, ranging from 'Sea Green' 9W-GYR (G H Engleheart pre-1930) to more recent introductions such as 'Blisland' 9W-YYR (R A Scamp 2000), 'Greenpark' 9W-GGO (Ballydorn Bulb Farm 1988) and 'Campion' and 'Patois' have been successful on the show bench but show little sign as yet of displacing 'Cantabile' and 'Killearnan'. 'Campion' and 'Patois' are both coded 9W-GYR and were raised by B S Duncan who registered them in 1980 and 1992 respectively.

The evolving definition of division 9

Division 9 was first defined in 1910 as "Poeticus varieties". In 1950, this definition gave way to the more restrictive wording "Characteristics of the *N. poeticus* group without admixture of any other". Whilst in principle this definition allowed the use of (say) one or even both parents from division 3, provided the resulting cultivar showed the characteristics of the *N. poeticus* group, it was in practice widely misinterpreted by hybridizers as meaning that division 9 cultivars could only be bred from members of the *N. poeticus* group or hybrids derived entirely from it. A potentially more flexible regime emerged in 1977 when the definition of division 9 became "Characteristics of *N poeticus* group predominant". However, in 1989 the definition of division 9 was again tightened to read "Characteristics of the *N. poeticus* group without admixture of any other: usually one flower to a stem; perianth segments pure white; corona usually disc-shaped, with a green or yellow centre and a red rim; flowers fragrant". In part because of concerns that the 1989 definition ignored the wholly orange or red coronas of some true poeticus, the definition of division 9 changed again by the RHS in 1998 and now reads: -

"Characteristics of the *N. poeticus* group: usually one flower to a stem; perianth segments pure white; corona very short or disc-shaped, usually with a green and/or yellow centre and a red rim, but sometimes of a single colour; flowers usually fragrant."

What is "different" about how we define division 9?

The horticultural classification of daffodils is based on appearance rather than parentage. This sensible approach reflects the difficulty of being certain about the parentage of daffodils, whether due to mistakes or open pollination. It is for this reason that the definitions of the species based divisions other than division 9 put so much stress on the "characteristics" of the underlying species (division 6), or Sections of the botanical classification (5, 7, 8 and 10), being "clearly evident". None-the-less, every "characteristic" of the underlying species is not expected to be present in their hybrids and within rather vague limits, some variation in one or more of size, form, poise or colour is common.

It will be clear from what has been said earlier that repeated attempts have been made to ensure that cultivars in division 9 not only have characteristics "clearly evident" but that they resemble the underlying *N. poeticus* group. Concern that hybrids in a species based division should be recognizably similar to the underlying species is not unique to division 9, as evidenced by debate in division 6. What is unique to division 9, is the extremes to which such concerns have been carried. For example, we permit hybrids in other species based divisions to be of any colour, yet remain very uneasy about the concept of division 9 cultivars with coronas coloured entirely green, white or pink, or which approach standard division 3 cultivars in size.

The consequences of our current approach to division 9

Two inevitable results flow from both past and present attitudes to division 9. First, as evidenced by some of our contributors, is the difficulty experienced by hybridizers trying to breed distinctive cultivars capable of displacing old favourites such as 'Cantabile'. Second, is the controversy that often surrounds any new cultivar that looks likely to break the mould. An example of this second point is provided by 'Killearnan'; which has been described as having the whiteness, scent and anthers of a division 9 cultivar, but the stem, neck, and poise of a division 3 cultivar. Many enthusiasts have argued that 'Killearnan' ought to be registered in division 3, but regard it as a fine large flower with a smooth perianth, which they none-the-less seem happy to grow and exhibit successfully in classes for division 9 cultivars.

Where next?
Another way of looking at the problem is to argue that the obvious evolutionary path of the *N. poeticus* group has always been primarily outside division 9. Historians of daffodil hybridizing have repeatedly claimed that the ultimate source of orange and red in modern daffodil cultivars lies within the *N. poeticus* group. Such species are also said to be central to the evolution of most cultivars in division 3 and many in division 2 and to have impacted not only on corona/perianth proportions, but also on perianth shape and smoothness. A probable implication of this perspective, is that any major relaxation of how we define division 9 might give us some interesting and different cultivars for a while, but could easily lead, via convergent evolution, to a merging of divisions 9 and 3.

My interpretation of the above discussion it that we can choose to define division 9 in a way which leaves its cultivars distinct from those in division 3, but which many hybridizers will find frustrating. Alternatively, we can choose to permit an era of experiment and run the very real risk of losing a distinctive inheritance. What is not clear, is the scale and direction of a viable middle path, which would provide scope for hybridizers, to produce a wider range of distinctive cultivars which rightly belong in division 9 and not elsewhere.

If further investigation of the *N. poeticus* group in the wild were to significantly widen the range of characteristics present in the species, it would then be difficult to argue that they should be excluded from their cultivated hybrids in division 9. However, such surprises are perhaps best regarded as possible rather than probable and as a bridge to be crossed if and when it happens. Equally, it is possible to argue that what we already know about the *N. poeticus* group provides evidence relevant to some current concerns. We know for example that wild populations include flowers which range in size between those of intermediate and standard daffodils in division 3 and which at least occasionally have coronas entirely coloured red. Conversely, to the best of my knowledge we do not yet have evidence of the existence of members of the *N. poetcus* group which normally have coronas coloured entirely green, white, or yellow, let alone pink. Until we have such evidence, the future of division 9 may be primarily about protecting and from time to time renewing a small but beautiful group of hybrid daffodils, so that their distinctiveness is not lost in the tidal wave of hybridizing.

Breeding activity
During the decade 1992-2001 inclusive 78 cultivars were registered in division 9 by 15 hybridizers. Of these hybridizers eight were from the United States of America, four from the United Kingdom, two from New Zealand and one from Australia. However, 43 of these cultivars were raised by Mrs. Merton S (Meg) Yerger from Maryland, who only briefly distributed a few of her bulbs. If Mrs Yerger's cultivars are excluded, we are left with 35 new cultivars, rather more than we noted in divisions 5 and 8 but significantly less than we found in divisions 6 and 7 over comparable ten-year periods.

Breeding needs and trends
In his article "Chromosome numbers in *Narcissus* cultivars and their significance to the plant breeder" (*New Plantsman* vol.14, December 1992) Peter Brandham investigated 38 cultivars in division 9. Given that 28 were diploids, nine were tetraploids and that there was only one triploid, it ought to be relatively easy to get viable seed from division 9 cultivars. This said, despite about a century of hybridizing, poeticus hybrids which flower before late in the season and which are sun-proof in bright weather remain rare. Consequently, it can be argued that even in respect of standard sized division 9 cultivars much remains to be done and may not be easy to achieve. Similarly, despite the apparently large number of diploid poeticus hybrids, miniature cultivars remain scarce. Ignoring several near misses, 'Crimson Rim' 9W-GGR (Leone Y Low 2000) and 'Haiku' 9W-GYR (raised by Murray Evans but registered in 2002 by Steven J Vinisky) are currently two of only a handful of potential miniature division 9 cultivars. Two possible explanations here are probably the lack of interest in miniature division 9 cultivars until relatively recently and the difficulty of breeding out tall stems once flower size has been reduced. Interestingly, division 9 cultivars registered during the last decade show a wide range of flower diameters with most of intermediate size, but four with diameters in the 86-93mm (3.4-3.8in) range. However, as will be seen from our cultivar surveys, several hybridizers are trying with some success to raise larger as well as traditional sized cultivars. Of the 15 hybridizers noted earlier, only Mrs M S Yerger registered poets during 1992-2001 which used members of the *N. poeticus* group as one of the parents. Given the substantial variability within the species, there is perhaps a case for hybridizers returning to basics in division 9 and Ron Scamp's attempts to do just that (see below) will no doubt be watched with great interest.

Lastly, we should not forget that the *N. poeticus* group and its hybrids in division 9 have been used extensively to improve the form and colour of hybrids in other species based divisions. We discussed Poetaz last year, and Alec Gray's 'Bebop', 'Bobbysoxer' and 'Clare' remind us of what can be achieved when using *N. poeticus* to breed division 7 hybrids. There is also the strong possibility that the short, broad, but curved and reflexing petals of some pink cultivars in division 6 may owe more to a distant poet ancestor than to *N. cyclamineus*.

POETICUS RAMBLINGS
RON SCAMP

Division 9 daffodils are those with the characteristics of the *N. poeticus* group. This very beautiful group of flowers is probably the most neglected in all the divisions, and for many years has not been given much attention by hybridizers in the United Kingdom.

For many years the finest we could offer were 'Cantabile' still one of the best for show or the garden and varieties such as 'Sea Green' a notoriously difficult one to keep and 'Pidget' a flower which has not received the recognition it deserves. 'Poet's Way' raised by Tom Bloomer was also a good advance and has many awards to it credit.

In latter years very few hybridizers have given much serious attention to the Poets, with the exception of the late Sir Frank Harrison who has raised an exceptional strain of deep green eyed varieties, and Brian Duncan, who has introduced 'Campion', 'Patois' and 'Lyric' in the traditional style, 'Vers Libre' which is a little larger than most and 'Dimple' with a solid red corona. Also from Northern Ireland is Kate Read, who has raised several poets with solid red coronas and recently registered 'Audrey Robinson' from seed sent to her by Arthur Robinson.

Seedling PDW/101 raised many years ago by P D Williams was grown on quite a big scale here in Cornwall but was only registered as 'Lady Serena' in 1976. 'Lady Serena' and the perhaps controversial 'Killearnan' from John Lea were both larger in size, and hold a string of awards to their credit.

Sadly the poets raised at Rosewarne have not made any impact, perhaps this is due to commercial reasons and to these cultivars not being given any public profile or exhibited at shows. There are however many fine cultivars where 'Lady Serena' and other poets have been used as parents. The CABGA hold stocks of some of these cultivars and may release them in the future.

For many years I have been acquiring the finest division 9 cultivars from all over the world. My plan is to experiment with these and species such as *N. poeticus physaloides* and *N. poeticus hellenicus* and some near poets, with a view to raising flowers which are a little larger than most older cultivars. Such introductions would be more acceptable to the flower market as well as for garden and show purposes. So far I have introduced 'Colville', 'Penjerrick' and 'Blisland' which are all a little larger in size and proving themselves both as show and garden flowers. I also have a considerable number of seedlings with more traditional form, some of which have almost solid green or red centres and have already made their mark as potential winners.

The opportunities for advancement in this division is great. However to successfully pollinate poeticus flowers it is essential to emasculate the blooms as soon as they open, i.e to remove the pollen bearing stamens before the pollen becomes loose. Otherwise the bloom is almost certain to self pollinate before the stigma is exserted.

Nothing can be more enjoyable at the end of a daffodil season than to relax with the poets and savour the beautiful colours and scent of these flowers.

I offer my sincere apologies to any hybridizer whose work I have in my ignorance omitted to mention, we would all love to see and enjoy your flowers.

SIR FRANK HARRISON'S RAISINGS
NIAL WATSON

Frank Harrison has been devoted to daffodils and in particular poeticus hybrids for over 50 years. Of all the Irish hybridizers he has contributed the most to this division and over the years has registered 21 cultivars.

He was very impressed with Guy Wilson's famous division 9, 'Cantabile' and this formed the basis for most of his breeding. He generally used 'Cantabile' as the seed parent and with Guy Wilson's 'Cushendall' 3W-GWW for pollen produced 'Moyle' 9W-GYO. This cultivar has a very green appearance and by crossing 'Moyle' with 'Cushendun' 3W-Y he produced 'Greenpark' 9W-GGO. Green coronas became his prime breeding objective. With 'Cantabile' as the seed parent and 'Moyle' for pollen he produced a range of extremely green coronas including 'Innishowen Head' 9W-GGO and 'Mizzen Head' 9W-GYY.

With such an intense programme of breeding he produced several spin-offs. An open pollinated 'Cantabile' hybrid gave him 'Red Hugh' 9W-GRR and spurred him on to develop a range of division 9s with orange or red coronas. There are still several unnamed seedlings waiting to be introduced. There was also a range of what can only be called all white division 9s although strictly speaking these are division 3. 'Fairy Footsteps' and 'Fairy Spell', both 3W-GGW, are in form and size division 9 but are of division 3 breeding. However, 'Canticle' 9W-GYR which can only be described as a vastly improved 'Cantabile' must be his most successful bloom on the show bench. Often misnamed as 'Cantabile' this flower has superb form, poise and substance. It has a rather long neck but it is strong enough to give it good poise.

Frank Harrison never achieved his goal of an all green corona but came very close with a seedling he called 'Green Tragedy'. He did not register the seedling as it was very ugly but it did have an all green corona of sorts! However, he did raise a borderline division 3 seedling that is probably diploid, which has a deep moss green cup with a very thin orange rim. The rim often has only orange flecks on it and is occasionally totally green.

Editors note. Sadly, after the above note was written and just as the Yearbook *was going to press, Sir Frank Harrison – who had gradually retired during the last couple of years – died on 13 August 2002 aged 92. We will publish an obituary in next year's edition.*

POETICUS HYBRIDS IN THE USA
MARY LOU GRIPSHOVER

The situation with poeticus hybrids in the United States of America is much the same as in most other countries. There are a limited number of registrations. That may be because, in large part, the definition of division 9 is somewhat limiting. However, to maintain the "look" of a poeticus, and the classification is based on looks, not genetics, that seems necessary. Perhaps we, as exhibitors and gardeners, need to expand our level of acceptance, so that we accept somewhat starry perianths as well as the broad, overlapping perianths, which seem to be preferred these days.

A reading of Bill Lee's "Introduction to 2001 Show Reports" in the September 2001 edition of *The Daffodil Journal* [Published by the American Daffodil Society (ADS)] shows that only 'Killearnan' appears in winning collections more than once - a total of seven times. Fourteen other cultivars appeared once each. Most enthusiasts would agree that 'Killearnan' doesn't "look" like a poet, but it is an excellent flower that blooms at the right time for many shows.

The ADS *Daffodil Data Bank* lists 146 poets registered by American hybridizers. Of these, eleven are from Mitsch/Havens and ten from the late Murray Evans. Nine amateur raisers account for an additional 19 cultivars, but it is Mrs. Merton Yerger who accounts for the vast majority of American registrations in this division - 106. However, her cultivars were not widely distributed. She put out a small list for a time, but most were never available commercially.

Most cultivars in division 9 have either an orange or red rim, with green and yellow in the other two-cup zones. However, two Mitsch cultivars, 'Tart' and 'Vienna Woods' (see Fig. 2) have solid red cups; while his 'Bon Bon' is coded 9 W-OOR. 'Bright Angel' and 'Emerald' are both 9 W-GOR. Though 'Quetzal' 9 W-GYR is a bit older, it is still a nice flower, and still seen on the show bench. The only other cultivars showing more than a rim of colour are Daniel Bellinger's 'Mary Oliver' 9 W-GOR, and Donna Dietsch's 'Maya Angelou' 9 W-GOO.

Leone Low has registered 'Crimson Rim' 9 W-GGR which has won prizes as a miniature. Murray Evans' 'Haiku', newly registered by Steve Vinisky, may also qualify as a miniature. Time will tell with both of these cultivars.

Five cultivars are attributed to Dr. William Bender. 'Dylan Thomas' 9 W-GYR has found limited distribution. 'Sea White', said to be a sport of 'Sea Green' is registered as 9 W-W. I wonder, does an all white flower "look" like a poet?

Helen Link has registered four cultivars, three of which found limited distribution in the Midwest Region of the ADS: 'Lucy Jane', 'Phebe' and 'Sheilah'.

Edwin C Powell registered three poets in the 1940s. Poet enthusiasts have rescued some of these, and Michael Berrigan has used 'Catawba' and 'Niantic' in winning collections in ADS shows during the last two years.

Bill Pannill, who has registered many fine flowers covering all the divisions, has only one registered in division 9: 'Omega' 9 W-YYR.

As evidenced by his entries at this year's ADS Annual Convention and National Show, Steve Vinisky has raised several poeticus seedlings and has made extensive use of members of the *N. poeticus* group in crosses involving division 9, and other divisions.

Poeticus hybrids are not difficult to produce. I have many nice flowers from a cross of

'Dactyl' × an Evans red-cupped poet seedling, one of which is named 'Ten of Diamonds'. (For you card players, yes, it was named to fill out a royal flush, as there's also an ace, king, queen, and knave of diamonds. I'd love to have them all and exhibit a collection sometime, but I'm missing the queen.) A sister seedling, 73-22-6, has won top prizes in local shows. In my climate, poets often set open pollinated seed. These, too, produce nice flowers. The problem is finding something distinctive.

NEW ZEALAND POETS
MAX HAMILTON

Poets are rarely seen on the show bench at North Island National shows because as a rule the shows are held mid-September. However, at the South Island shows held at the end of September we have had up to 13 entries in the single bloom class.

I feel that the old requirement of having to have both parents poets before they were accepted for registration (but see p.21) plus their inherited late to very late flowering season and of course their slow rate of increase have all contributed to their not being so popular among exhibitors and breeders. Then exhibitors have to cope with their dislike of being lifted and given hot water treatment and the lack of rainfall in some of our drier areas. Yet left alone you often see poets in abandoned gardens flowering year after year so they are survivors.

We have had some keen growers trying their hand at breeding poets despite knowing that their late flowering genetic inheritance would prevent the results from being seen at most shows.

In the 1940s A H Ahrens bred 'Rondo' with the stock ending up with Ron Hyde who registered it in 1958. Jack Leitch took over Ahrens's stocks after his death in 1945 continued breeding and registered 'Dreamland'. Both these cultivars have proved to be very good breeders. 'Dreamland' was a smallish very neat flower on a very tall stem for a poet.

Ken Farmer from Rotorua produced 'Gweal' which he registered in 1978. I use 'Gweal' as a seed parent as it has a good bulb, strong growing habits for a poet, a large flower, around 90mm (3.6in) in diameter, which these days wouldn't get on to the show bench. However I feel it is worth trying to impart 'Gweal's vigour and bulb size to its progeny.

I presume the 'Cantata' raised by Ted Coller of Christchurch was the one used by Maurice Butcher in his efforts to raise new cultivars. 'Embee' was bred from a seedling crossed with ('Cantata' × 'Rondo') and 'Sam Hunt' from the cross 'Rupert Brooke' with 'Rondo'. Both of these were registered by Alf Chappell who acquired the stock after Maurice's death.

Mavis Verry also tried her hand and with her usual generosity gave me three seedlings to try in 1984, some of which she identified as early flowering. John Hunter was another recipient who has kept on breeding, exchanging seedlings with Denise McQuarrie. Denise has had Best Bloom division 9 at the Te Anau South Island National Show with a seedling bred from 'Rondo' × 'Cantabile'. Denise was very generous and gave me the flower to bring back home. Seedlings from its pollen onto my own seedlings should flower in 2002.

Isobel Dreaver of Owaka was another who when she gave up growing daffodils gave her stocks of seedling poets to Ron Abernethy to grow on. Ron has registered three; both 'Izzy's Gem' and 'Catlin Jewel' have fully red cups.

Colin Crotty who is also trying his hand, says that when displayed to the public, the flowers create a lot of interest and he finds it hard to keep up with the demands for bulbs.

My own efforts go way back to the sixties when I first got a bulb of 'Dreamland' and a seedling from Jack Leitch. To date 'Tino Pai' which has several Premier Poet in show awards to its credit is the best I have shown, . I have an early flowering sister seedling which if left down will flower mid-September. From 'Moyle' × seedling there are several very nice seedlings some with cups that have very deep green eyes and primrose yellow cups with no red or orange. Other crosses using my own seedlings have given flowers with full red cups, and others with pure white coronas and deep green eyes. They give me a lot of pleasure at the end of the season around mid-October, although they flower too late for the shows.

Now that I have a very good collection with my own seedlings, the best obtainable here in New Zealand and stocks imported from Great Britain, the United Sates of America and Tasmania my intentions are to endeavour to breed earlier flowering poets with good vigour, plant habits and larger bulbs.

There may be others who are trying to breed that I haven't seen on the show benches here and if so all I can do is wish them well in their efforts.

DIVISION 9 IN AUSTRALIA
RICHARD PERRIGNON

It is now 75 years or so since Lubbe and Sons of Lisse registered the Dutch tetraploid 'Actaea'. Since then, it has been much used by Australian daffodil breeders in the production of standard division 3 cultivars. Unfortunately, the same cannot be said of its use in the development of Poeticus hybrids here - that is, hybrids expressing predominantly the morphological characteristics of *Narcissus poeticus* - which has met with comparative neglect. There are a number of likely reasons. First, like their overseas counterparts, Australian breeders have traditionally focussed mainly on the holy grail of the larger, more geometrically perfect standard cultivar, often at the expense of interest in species and their F1 hybrids. Secondly, division 9 cultivars tend to bloom late in the season, often in October or even November, thus requiring a long, cool Spring to flower well. Most of the Australian gardening population live in coastal mainland cities, where heat waves can be expected as early as October, effectively precluding optimal culture of *N. poeticus* and its offspring. There is another, lesser-known factor. Rainfall in temperate Australia tends to favour the Summer months, and to fall off dramatically in late Spring, just when these bulbs need to stock up on water and nutrients to increase in size, multiply and survive the dormant period. It is not difficult to see why they should do poorly in areas where their flowering is met with comparative drought.

Whatever the reasons for this apparent neglect, there are nevertheless one or two Australian cultivars that qualify for entry into the elite club of division 9. By far the best is 'Ringer' 9W-GYR. This fine show cultivar was bred by Rod Barwick of Glenbrook Bulb Farm from 'Ypsilante' × 'Bright Angel'. Its perianth is a glistening white, and its petals are slightly rounded and incurved. This is not the "starched collar" perianth so beloved by Tassie breeders, but rather a bloom which exhibits the grace of its species forbears, in the best tradition of division 9. The flat cup has a green eye with bright yellow surround, the rim etched in bright red. It is earlier flowering than many of its kind - mid October in Tasmania, and late September in warmer climes, making it useful for the show bench. It has enjoyed a rewarding career on the show bench since at least 1988, and continues to amass awards.

For anyone looking for a good show cultivar in this division, a bulb or two of 'Ringer' should prove a good investment.

NARCISSUS POETICUS IN THE GARDEN
CHRISTINE SKELMERSDALE

The sight, and indeed the scent of the dainty flowers of *N. poeticus recurvus*, with their tiny red eyes peeping through the grass like the pheasant's eyes of its common name is, for me, inextricably mixed with the fruit blossom and tulips of late spring.

The red-rimmed cup and the reflexed white perianth of *N. poeticus recurvus* must be one of the best known and instantly recognized of all daffodils. It was introduced into this country towards the end of the 19th century and its late flowering –usually in May – coupled with its strong perfume guaranteed it almost instant popularity; a popularity that has continued among gardeners, despite the rather weak form of its flowers.

Although *N. recurvus* can be grown in a border its rather lax habit and iron constitution make it an ideal subject for naturalizing in grass. Unlike most daffodils it does not need to be planted in dense drifts. A scattering of them among earlier varieties will effectively disguise the dying foliage of their predecessors. A definite case of less is more. The taller and more robust hybrid, 'Actaea', is equally effective in similar situations although it is earlier flowering.

One of the most common problems with this group in the garden is unexpected blindness. The principal reason for this is their naturally late flowering period, which in this country often seems to coincide with a period of warm dry weather. The sunshine may be welcomed by those enjoying the garden but unless there is an unbroken supply of moisture the poetius daffodils will abort their flowers and concentrate their efforts on producing a new bulb for the following year. On the nursery here one year 300 'Pheasant's Eye' buds earmarked for the Chelsea Flower Show were all aborted during a sudden hot dry spell in early May. A timely application of water would have saved them. They therefore do best in moist soils in an open situation where they are not shaded by trees, although even here some supplementary watering may be necessary.

The late flowering of most of the poeticus hybrids makes them a valuable addition to the garden. Their stiff habit, with the crisp red eye staring out of a perfectly round ruff of glistening white petals means they are probably more suited to the border. They should be planted towards the front or they will be hidden by the burgeoning herbaceous plants. Here their more perfect flower shape can easily be appreciated and they form good, long lasting clumps. 'Cantabile' and 'Chesterton' (see Fig. 3) are reliable hybrids and in common with 'Actaea' are the only division 9 hybrids to have received an Award of Garden Merit. All are also excellent cut flowers, although in common with other red-cupped cultivars they are prone to "burn".

Although classified as a division 4 (double) 'Tamar Double White' should be included here as it is the double form of the 'Pheasant's Eye' daffodil. The remains of the red edged cup is just visible among the massed white perianth segments, and it shares the same distinctive perfume. It also shares the same proclivity to blindness in dry situations and should therefore be planted in a border that is not prone to excessive dryness. Discreet staking may also be necessary as the flower heads are rather heavy and can tend to flop.

Although division 9 narcissus are, by their definition, very similar to each other they are among the most distinctive and attractive groups for the garden.

The Canadian Tulip Festival and World Tulip Summit

James Akers

In the Second World War, members of the Netherlands royal family sought refuge in Canada, during which time Princess Margriet was born in Ottawa. Canadian soldiers were also heavily involved in the liberation of Holland and many lost their lives and are buried there. In recognition of the support that they had received, the people of Holland sent, in the autumn of 1945, a gift of 100,000 tulip bulbs to be planted in Ottawa, followed in 1946 by a further 20,000 bulbs sent by Princess Juliana. Each year a further 10,000 bulbs are sent to Ottawa by the Queen's household. The tulip flowers were greatly admired from the beginning and in 1953 it was decided to hold the first Canadian Tulip Festival, founded by the world famous photographer Malak Karsh. The festival grew quickly so that it has now become the largest tulip festival in the world.

This 50th Anniversary in 2002 was marked with many special events including a World Tulip Summit with speakers from many parts of the world. Unfortunately Malak died in 2001, but the festival held from 3 to 20 May was dedicated to his memory and given the theme "Tulipmania! Tulips like you've never seen them before".

Tulip plantings

Several million bulbs were planted over a 15km (10 mile) Canada Tulip Route with 21 Official Sites that could be seen from Tulip Shuttle buses, free to travellers each weekend during the festival. Outstanding among these was Commissioners Park where 300,000 tulips were planted, accompanied by displays recording the history of the "Gift of Tulips". Malak was commemorated by a special garden at Maison du Citoyen, Gatineau. Virtually every large store and shop in the cities of Ottawa and Gatineau featured tulips in their window displays and every school, business and individual resident that wished to participate had planted tulips to mark the 50th Anniversary.

Major's Hill Park

Most of the events associated with the Festival took place in Major's Hill Park in the centre of Ottawa, close to the parliamentary buildings. These included a pop-concert that attracted an audience of around 6,000 people and an art exhibition designed and constructed by Canadian artists and featuring live tulips. All the exhibits had individual themes, many in a traditional manner such as "Tulip Carpet" by Adrian Göllner in the style of a Turkish Carpet. Others like "[trans]plant" by NIP Paysage, a 30m (100ft) long assembly of 200 transparent tubes holding growing tulips including the bulb and roots suspended in liquid, would have been worthy contestants for a Turner Prize. My personal favourite was "No Bed of Roses" by Anne Swannell with all the bedding constructed from individual tulips supported by a brass bed-frame. The thousands of flowers specially grown for the art displays were delivered to the park in hundreds of cardboard cartons. Unfortunately when opened these revealed immature, small flowers which in the prevailing cold weather took several days to reach their peak.

Also within the park was an International Friendship Village with exhibits from several countries, including Holland, Japan, Turkey and the USA, many of which included food and drink that was a speciality of the country. From the United Kingdom, Spalding Flower Parade had a superb parade float decorated with silk tulips which attracted much attention and the Royal Oak British Pub provided food and music with a Celtic theme; their range of imported draught beers proved very popular.

Also popular was "Artisans in the Park" where, in a 1,400 square metre (15,000 square foot) tent, 125 artisans displayed for sale handmade products such as jewellery, paintings and pottery, the majority of which had a tulip theme.

Commemorative stamps and coin
To coincide with the 50th Anniversary, Canada Post issued four domestic rate commemorative stamps. These featured the tulip cultivars 'City of Vancouver', 'Monte Carlo', 'Ottawa' and 'The Bishop' in the background of which are shown respectively, the Vancouver skyline, tulip beds at Ottawa's Dow's Lake, the Canadian War Memorial and Ottawa's Civic Hospital, birthplace of Princess Margriet.

"Celebrating the flower that transformed Canada's national capital", the Royal Canadian Mint struck 20,000 commemorative "Golden Tulip Coins" – one for each of the bulbs that Princess Juliana gave to Canada more than five decades ago. This very attractive 50-cent sterling silver coin shows in gold relief a tulip and the year 2002 and on the reverse in silver relief the head of Queen Eizabeth II.

The World Tulip Summit
It was the idea of the Festival Organiser Michel Gauthier to hold a World Tulip Summit during the 50th Anniversary. A great tulip enthusiast and avid collector and reader of tulip books Michel was aware of the Great Tulip Conference of the Royal National Tulip Society, held at the *Royal Botanic Society's Gardens*, Regents Park, London on 12 May 1897. His aim was to hold the second great conference and accordingly tulip specialists from around the world were invited to attend the summit that took place at the Château Laurier Hotel, Ottawa on Friday to Sunday, 10-12 May 2002.

First day
HRH Princess Margriet of the Netherlands officially opened the conference on the Friday morning by unveiling the Royal Canadian Mint's Golden Tulip Coin.

The first keynote speaker Anna Pavord, introduced by Sir Andrew Burns, British High Commissioner to Canada, spoke on the topic: The Tulip, *a book about the story of a flower that has made men mad*. In the limited time available, Anna gave personal anecdotes around some of the written words from her book which has received world-wide praise.

The conference then split into two or three parallel seminars. This was the most disappointing aspect of the conference because as each speaker spoke only on one occasion, delegates were forced to make a very difficult choice of which talk to attend. The organisers intend to offset part of this problem by publishing in greater detail the content of each of the talks given but it will not fully compensate for missing hearing the speaker live. I can only record therefore details of the talks that I personally attended. For the morning seminar I chose to hear Dr William (Bill) B Miller, Professor of Horticulture at the University of Cornell, USA speak on the topic: *The Latest Research on Tulips*. Bill outlined the setting up of the Flower Bulb Research Institute at the university, whose sponsors include the Royal Dutch Exporters Association for Flower Bulbs and Nursery Stock. In order to capture the contract from the previous holders a large investment in the latest technology was necessary. Bill spoke at length about the research carried out into the methods of packaging tulips and other bulbs to prevent them from coming into growth while still in the container in which they are sold. Isao Imai, Deputy Mayor of Tonami, Japan and Yasuji Miyazaki conducted the parallel seminar whose topics were

Celebration of Tonami Tulip Fair and *Floating Tulips and the Tulip Industry in Japan.*

During lunch two of the artists, France Cormier and Anne Swannell, spoke about the methods they had used in the creation of their art exhibit described above.

For the first afternoon session I chose David Norton, Chief Executive of Springfield Gardens and Chairman of the Spalding Flower Parade. David used old photographs to relate the history of the bulb growing industry in Lincolnshire and the effect that the great growth in visitor numbers to see the bulbs in flower and the parade had on the local economy and infrastructure. David also outlined the cuurent plans for redevelopment of the Springfield Gardens. Parallel seminars were given by Sonia Day, a British born Canadian writer whose new book is reviewed on page 67 on the topic *From Monet to Malak: tulip lovers throughout history* and Douglas Cardinal, a Canadian architect.

The final seminar on the first day was conducted by Mark Cullen, a radio and television host and writer who spoke about a number of visits he had made to Europe in *Garden Inspiration from Britain and Holland*.

After the completion of the day's events, the delegates were invited to the dedication ceremony of the new Tulip Peace Garden at which the plaque was unveiled by Princess Margriet.

Second day
The opening keynote address was given by Wendy Peleman, Area Manager USA/Canada & Far East at the International Flower Bulb Centre in the Netherlands on *Tulip Trends in North America and Asia*. Wendy described in great detail the research that had been undertaken to identify the different customer requirements within these markets and the effect that style changes, fashion and reduction in garden size had on the product that was supplied. Of all the talks given over the two days this was the one that created the most discussion from the floor of the conference, with several comments that the danger of such an approach was that there would be a significant reduction in the choice of tulip cultivars available for purchase and particularly in the range of colours.

Dr. Selma Akyyazici Özkoçak Lecturer at Boðaziçi University, Department of History, Turkey then spoke about *The History of Tulips*. An architect by profession Dr. Özkoçak is particularly interested in the interactions between buildings and their urban and natural settings. Her studies of old manuscripts provided a fascinating insight into the way in which formal gardens in Turkey were planted many centuries ago, most of which of course featured tulips.

The parallel seminar was given by Janet Rosenberg on *The Show Must Go On-The In and Outs of Exhibition Garden Design*.

In the second morning seminar, representing the RHS with *Tulips in the United Kingdom – the 19th and 20th Centuries*, I started with details of the work done on tulips at The John Innes Institute, Merton under the directorship of Sir Daniel Hall during which time the cause of colour breaking in tulips was identified. I then went on to describe the role of the RHS over 50 years in the production of the *Classified Register of Tulip names* until it was handed over to the Netherlands, and current allocation of Award of Garden Merit to tulips. My talk finished with the history of the English Florists' Tulip and the Wakefield and North of England Tulip Society. I was able to present Michel Gauthier with a copy of the original booklet, produced by Peter Barr, of the talks given at the 1897 conference for his collection. Given the earliness of the season I was able to take to Canada four rectified flowers, three of which, 'Lord Stanley' flamed and feathered and 'Mabel' flamed would also have been on display at the first conference, thus fulfilling the theme "Tulips like you have never seen them before".

The parallel seminar *Capture the emotion of the tulip* was conducted by Monique Martin a Canadian artist from Saskatchewan who specialises in tulip paintings. I gave the four florists' tulips to Monique to paint and although one was stolen, she has now completed three paintings and hopes to do more in future years.

The luncheon speaker was Ed Lawrence whose theme was the *History of Gardens in the National Capital Region – Ottawa*. Ed has for the past sixteen years been one of the foremost gardening experts on Canadian radio and television programmes and has won several awards. He was responsible for the 12,000 square feet of greenhouses at the Governor General's residence Rideau Hall and is now in charge of both the grounds and greenhouses for all six official residences in the National Capital Region, including that of the Prime Minister.

The first afternoon seminar on *The Species Tulip* was given by broadcaster and author Larry Hodgson, who is President of the Canadian Garden Writers Association. Larry expressed his regret at the difficulty growers have in obtaining a range of truly named tulip species in North America or by importing from specialist growers in Europe.

The first parallel seminar *History of tulip beds in Ottawa* was conducted by Sherry Berg, a landscape architect who is responsible for the design of the tulip and other displays in the 60 federal and park sites around the National Capital Region.

The second seminar was conducted jointly by Jean-Claude Mari, Deputy Mayor of Nice, France and Cathy Winters the manager of the Floriade – Canberra Tulip Festival in Australia; the topics were *Bataille de fleurs, France* and *Flor, Australia*.

The final seminar of the conference was conducted by Anna Pavord, unexpectedly because she believed that she was only giving the opening address, on the subject of her latest book *Plant Partners*. *

The second day ended with the closing dinner at which the Poet Laureate Michel Therein read the poem that he had written to commemorate the Summit and 50th Anniversary.

Third Day
The final Sunday morning of the conference was taken up by a garden tour of Ottawa and the National Capital Region conducted by Ed Lawrence and including Commissioners Park, Maple Lawn, Mackenzie Estates and Rideau Hall. In addition we were invited to Earnscliffe where we were met by Sir Andrew and Lady Burns. Since 1930 successive United Kingdom High Commissions in Ottawa have lived at Earnscliffe, a Victorian house in grey stone on the south bank of the Ottawa River, which Sir John A. Macdonald, first Prime Minister of Canada owned and lived in for several years before his death there in 1891.

Canadian Tulip Festival and Future Summits
Plans have already begun for next year's event when the Canadian Tulip Festival will celebrate "G'day Australia – Tulips Down Under" from 2 to 19 May, 2003. Details of this and the event may be found on the very comprehensive web-site http://www.tulipfestival.ca

The view was expressed by Michel Gauthier and other delegates that a World Tulip Summit should be held every few years possibly in association with the many Tulip Festivals that are now held in both hemispheres.

* *Plant Partners* by Anna Pavord. Dorling Kindersley Limited, London 2001 £16.99

THE NOMENCLATURE OF SPECIES TULIPS

JOHN PAGE

In recent years I have found myself increasingly drawn to species tulips and in order to find out more about them I tried to include a specialist on the subject in a one-day bulb conference I was putting together for the Alpine Garden Society. Some candidates were simply unavailable, but a greater number were clearly shying away from the topic and when I probed further for the reasons behind their reluctance it became apparent that the systematics of species tulips (what I wanted to know more about) was a path along which they were not prepared to tread on a public platform. At a more practical level as I delved further, staff whom I interviewed at one major garden were loath to plant tulips amongst the rockwork partly because they were genuinely not sure what they were growing. Similarly, in a well-known botanic garden, where a number of species of tulip were being grown, the staff were to some extent still relying for purposes of identification on Volume 5 of the *Flora Europaea*, but that deals with only eleven species from our continent and three related taxa from the eastern boundaries of Europe. The great bulk of the tulip species whose centre of distribution is Central Asia were of course ineligible for inclusion in this work. It is perhaps not surprising then that no volunteer from amongst the professionals would come forward for the planned bulb conference and in the end, having photographed tulips in many parts of the Mediterranean, Greece and Turkey and having grown a number of them both in the alpine house and the open garden, I gave part of the lecture myself. What follows is what I discovered in the process about the names and the difficulties of identification.

It is instructive to compare the situation in tulip nomenclature with that for the genus crocus. For a hundred years or more, George Maw's great Victorian monograph *The Genus Crocus* supplemented by E A Bowles' *A Handbook of Crocus and Colchicum* (1924) was the enthusiast's bible. In 1982, Brian Mathew published his superb update *The Crocus*, which he has further revised this very year in two numbers of *The Plantsman* (New Series. Vol 1, parts 1 and 2) and, taken together, these give us a key we can rely on. A gardener with a good knowledge of the morphology of this genus can be reasonably sure that he has the right name. This confidence on the part of growers is perhaps one of the reasons why the recent RHS Crocus Conference was so well attended. There is clearly great interest in cultivating many of the species. No such state of the art overall scheme of identification accessible to the general public in the form of a monograph exists for species tulips, and it is probably no coincidence that their cultivation appears to be languishing. The picture, however, may not be as dark as it first appears, as we shall see.

E Regel, Superintendent at St Petersburg Botanic Garden, published in 1873 the first review of the genus. J G Baker of Thirsk produced a synopsis of the genus a year later, which Pierre Edmond Boissier of Geneva revised in 1882. The significance of Boissier's work is that he reduced the classification of tulips to two sections, *Leiostemones* and *Eriostemones,* a dualism that survived throughout the twentieth century. W R Dykes' posthumously published *Notes on the Tulip Species* (1930) is our earliest decent attempt to study the less well-known members of the genus. He is best known of course for his work on Iris and he seems to have realized from the outset that tulips were a very different proposition. He is reported as saying that if he lived to the age of Methuselah he might be able to say something definite about the species and wild forms, but not until then. Overlapping him we find Sir A Daniel Hall whose beautifully researched and very comprehensive monograph *The Genus Tulipa* published by the RHS appeared shortly after the outbreak of the Second World War. Zinaida Botschantzeva's excellent *Tulips* (translated some twenty years later by H Q Varekamp and published by A A Balkema of Rotterdam in 1982) expanded our knowledge of the Central Asian species considerably. *Tulipa vvedenskyi* commemorates A I Vedenskii who contributed the section on Tulips to Volume 4 of the 1935 "*Flora of the Soviet Union*", translated into English some 30 yeras later. The 1949 edition of the RHS *Daffodil and Tulip Yearbook* contains his "*Key to the Tulips of the USSR*". In her book, Botschantzeva, in whose honour incidentally Vvedenskii named *Tulipa zenaidae*, described his approach to arranging tulips as grouping together species "according to their degree of affinity", e.g. those which shared the same degree of hairiness of the bulb tunic or flower shape or lacked a basal blotch. Anna Pavord's *The Tulip*, published by Bloomsbury of London in 1999, which has rightly enjoyed best-seller status for her presentation of the history of the tulip in cultivation, includes a chapter on the species which necessarily draws heavily on Hall and Botschantzeva.

These authors frequently refer to the extreme difficulty with which a taxonomist who tackles the genus is faced. Hall concluded, "It is impossible to construct a key for the genus that shall be proof against error, in some cases because of the variations to which a species is subject. In other cases the key can only lead to a sub-group in which the characteristics of the species are confused, e.g. the *humilis-pulchella-violacea* group, or in which the species can only be differentiated by a comparison of many features, e.g. the triploids of the *Oculus-solis* group". The remarkable variation in flower colour that can occur within a species was seized upon by the early breeders. In Gerard's *Herbal* which first appeared in 1597 we read under the heading tulip that this "strange and forrein floure each year bringeth forth new plants in sundry colours not seen before, all of which to describe were to roll Sisyphus stone or number the sands...Nature seeming to play more with this floure than with any other that I do know". What occurs in captivity is just as rampant in nature, with all the attendant problems for those who would identify the tulips they have found. Robert Rolfe summarised this nicely in an *Alpine Garden Society Bulletin* article: "Those who have studied the genus have tended to find that the few certainties they harboured soon collapse when trying to match plants and names in the field". No wonder then that professional horticulturalists (in the following instance Kenneth Beckett) are very much on their guard when faced with the task of describing a tulip, a caution well caught in the following extracts from Volume 2 of the AGS *Encyclopaedia of Alpines*: "*T. boeotica*... Closely allied to *T. undulatifolia* and sometimes sunk into it". "*T. doerfleri*... Close to *T. orphanidea* but darker red: perhaps conspecific". "*T. dubia*... Akin to *T. kaufmanniana*, but somewhat smaller...". "*T. ferganica*... Similar to *T. dubia* but leaves usually more deeply waved...". "*T. schrenkii*...Presumably it merits no more than varietal rank under *T. armena*". "*T. tschimganica*... sometimes adjacent to *T. greigii* and *T. kaufmanniana* with which it hybridises". "*T. tubergeniana*... Closely related to *T. fosteriana* and *T. lanata* and perhaps conspecific".

The case of the name *Tulipa gesneriana* is an interesting study in this context. Hall used the specific name "in a restricted sense for the crimson-scarlet tulips found in many localities in Asia Minor". In the *Flora Europaea* it denotes a locally naturalized, complex species or group found mainly in South West Europe from which most garden tulip cultivars have been derived. There is no known counterpart in Hall's areas of origin which matches those in the *Flora Europaea*, the assumption being that there was a huge influx of imports of Central Asian tulips into Europe from the fifteenth century onwards, from which a whole range of variants were selected and reselected resulting in a wide range of forms and colours. By contrast with Hall, the *Flora Europaea* gives the perianth colour as "scarlet, orange, yellow or purplish, sometimes broken". This European complex is often referred to as *Neo-tulipae*. Authorities over the years have accorded them in many instances specific status, but Hall downgraded his list of thirty or so *Neo-Tulipae* as plants with a common ancestor which were "species of doubtful validity". Anna Pavord gives the name very short shrift. "*T. gesneriana*: The collective name that Linnaeus gave in 1753 to a miscellaneous group of old cultivars". However, in the most recent major contribution to tulip systematics, as we shall see later, the name is back in favour.

Under normal circumstances, colour range is of relatively little importance to the taxonomist; who are more interested in structural features where more striking differences may be found. We have seen already, however, that in the case of tulips, colour matters greatly. Where else does the taxonomist look? Boissier's fundamental division of tulips into *Eriostemones* and *Leiostemones* derives from the fact that the former have hairs on the basal part of the filaments, whereas those of the latter are hairless. A minute difference one might think, but clearly it has been an essential starting-point for botanists for a very long time. What this reflects is that bulbs in particular, because they have such a relatively simple structure, are a great challenge to taxonomists. Traditionally, they have relied on five main structural features for purposes of identifying tulips. In addition to filament bases and colour, where the presence or absence of a central blotch is also an important diagnostic feature, they examine the bulb tunic (hairy inside or smooth), the flower profile (bowl-, cup-, funnel-shaped and does

the flower have a waist above the base for example) finally the leaves in terms of the number, colour, position on the stem etc.

Since 1997, we have had a further revision of tulip nomenclature which has swept away this reliance on the five criteria and we may now at long last have the basis for the kind of reliable overall survey of tulips similar to that which we possess for crocus and for which gardeners are crying out. I am referring to the paper "The Systematics of the Genus *Tulipa* L." by L W D Van Raamsdonk, W. Eikelboom, T De Vries and Th P Straathof of the DLO-Centre for Plant Breeding and Reproduction Research, Wageningen, Holland given at the 1997 International Symposium on Flower Bulbs. The authors have lumped the genus into approximately 55 species in a revision based on morphological and cytogenetical characteristics and relying heavily on data of geographical distribution; which for tulips in particular makes very good sense. The five criteria then have gone, to be replaced by analysis of variation of no less than 35 morphological characters of tulips in the section *Eriostemones*, and 34 in *Tulipa* subgenus *Tulipa* which replaces *Leiostemones*. *Tulipa gesneriana* is placed in the section *Tulipa* of this latter genus[1].

In addition to this highly significant work of the Dutch team we know that there is great interest in species tulips elsewhere, e.g. at Cambridge Botanic Garden, Dushanbe Botanic Garden in Tajikistan, the Gothenburg Botanical Institute and of course Kew. Is it too much to hope that some day soon from amongst them they will produce that new monograph that gardeners seek? As I suggested earlier, the cultivation of species tulips needs a boost and the surge of interest that we have seen in the growing of snowdrops, for example, which has resulted from the excellent new publications on *Galanthus*, could so easily be repeated.

[1] A taxonomic presentation of the genus *tulipa*, which appeared on page 33 of *Daffodils and Tulips 1997-8* as part of an article "Tulip Breeding at CPRO-DLO" by Th.P(Dolf) Straathof and Wim Eikelboom is reproduced overleaf.

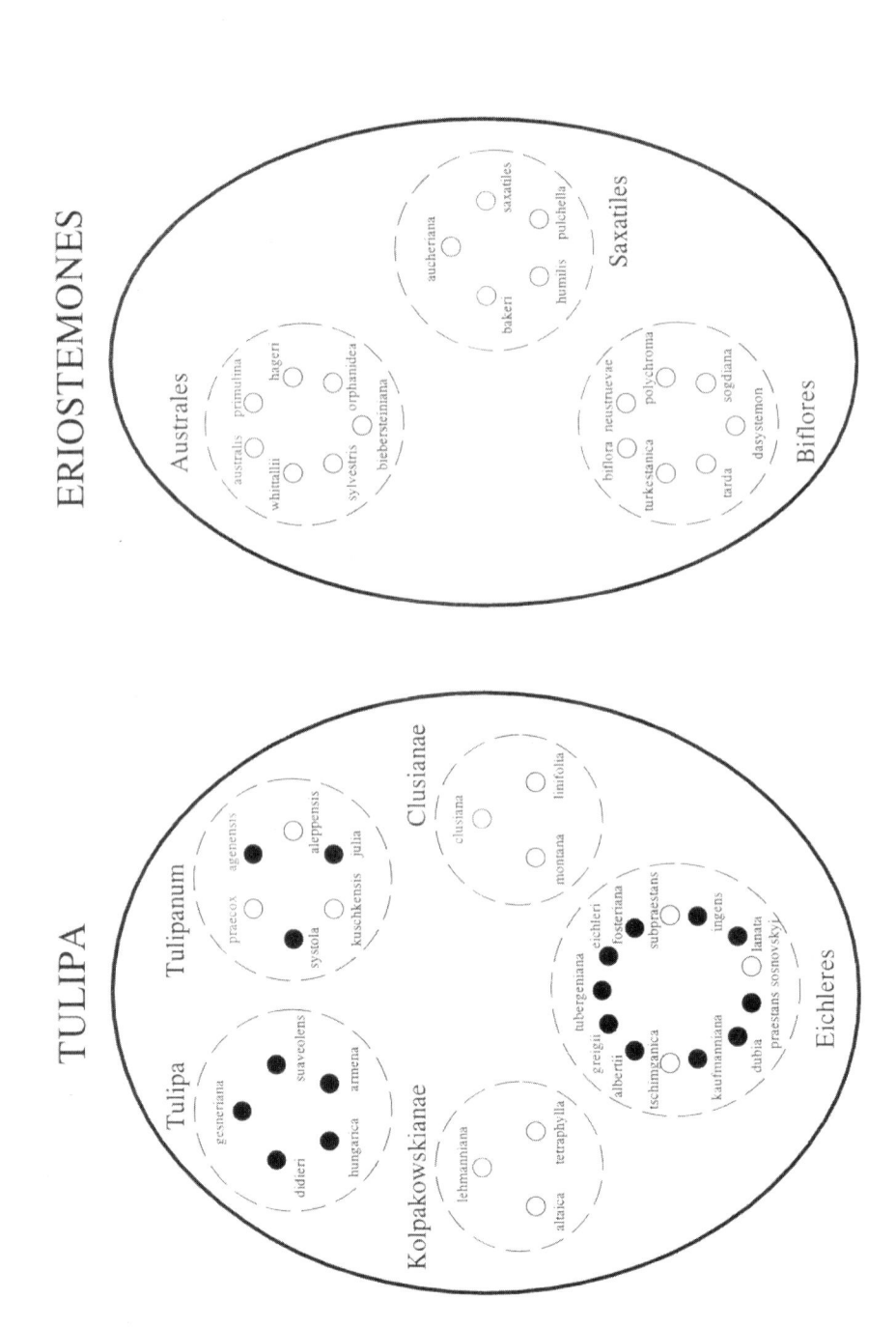

Daffodil, Snowdrop and Tulip Yearbook 2002-2003

Taxonomic presentation of the genus Tulipa. Filled dots are species from which interspecific hybrids with T. gesneriana are obtained. (Reproduced from Daffodil and Tulip Yearbook 1997-8, p.33)

Vintage Doubles

Sally Kington

The opportunity was recently taken to look at a quantity of double trumpet daffodils of the sort which have been in cultivation for a long time in the British Isles or have become naturalised. It arose when a news story ran in 1995 about a double daffodil flowering for the first time in living memory at the National Trust's Gibside estate near Newcastle upon Tyne. The picture in the paper did not look much like a daffodil. Yet people all over the country recognized it, and nearly two hundred reports of similar daffodils, many with pictures or specimens attached, were sent in to the Royal Horticultural Society (RHS). They came from more than sixty different counties in England, Wales, Scotland and Northern Ireland; they spoke of plants in old gardens "where they have always been", in gardens where they had suddenly appeared after clearance of the ground, in old orchards, in country estates, in churchyards and in woods. And at first glance, most of them appeared to be *Narcissus* 'Telamonius Plenus', in all its reputed variation.

The name Telamonius grandiplenus was given by A H Haworth in 1819 to one of the two double forms described by him of a yellow trumpet daffodil he had dubbed Ajax telamonius. He later identified T. grandiplenus with the daffodil John Parkinson had published in the early 17c as Pseudonarcissus aureus Anglicus maximus, or "Mr Wilmers great double Daffodill" (**1**). (*Note: The numbers in bold are to distinguish between the different daffodils mentioned here*).

In 1862, Peter Barr, Covent Garden nurseryman with a particular interest in identifying the old daffodils growing in English gardens, followed up Haworth by giving the name 'Van Sion' (Pseudo-Narcissus) to the one double yellow trumpet daffodil that he had in an early catalogue. This too was a reference to Mr Wilmer's Daffodil, for it echoed Parkinson's remark that Vincent Sion (originally from Flanders) should have been given the credit for introducing it into this country, not Wilmer. However, ten years after that, Barr deferred to Haworth and changed the name to 'Telamonius Plenus'.

It was probably a Barr-approved 'Telamonius Plenus' that F W Burbidge illustrated in *The Narcissus: its history and culture*, the authoritative work he co-authored with J G Baker in 1875. He referred to Barr in the Introduction as "an enthusiastic cultivator, who possesses perhaps the most complete collection of species and varieties in Europe."

The daffodil that people knew as 'Telamonius Plenus' from Barr's time on was the common double daffodil of gardens and orchards (to quote from Burbidge 1875); was common at Florence, "from whence it may be supposed it was introduced into this country" (Barr 1884); was also found in the south of France (Wolley-Dod 1890). It was very common in old gardens (Henslow 1910); it was the form commonly grown (Backhouse 1912); it was "king of the orchard" (Slinger 1935). It was said to be very variable, and of the two blooms illustrated in Burbidge (1875), one is trumpet-like, with the corona entire and the corona filled with numerous extra segments, some reflecting the form and colour of the perianth segments and some the corona; the other is mop-headed, with the corona split open and the segments within it loosened out and spreading. Barr (1884) spoke of the long-trumpet double Telamonius "in all its gradations."

The daffodils reported to the RHS in the wake of the Gibside story seemed to be a

37

measure of how variable 'Telamonius Plenus' was and how widespread it had become in the British Isles. However, before concluding that they did represent 'Telamonius Plenus' and 'Telamonius Plenus' alone, it seemed wise to consider what other double forms of *N. pseudonarcissus* had also been in cultivation over the centuries and might yet be found among them.

Reverting to Barr: in 1872, when he was first listing 'Telamonius Plenus' under that name, he remarked in addition on the probable existence of a double form of the *N. pseudonarcissus* of woods. He identified it with that which Parkinson called Pseudonarcissus Anglicus flore pleno, or "Gerrards Double Daffodill" (2). And two years later, he was able to write that he had succeeded in re-introducing it into cultivation: "this rare native Narcissus" that he listed as Pseudo-Narcissus plenus, golden trumpet, sulphur perianth. Burbidge (1875) said that Barr's bulbs were from the Isle of Wight, where Parkinson himself had said it was "naturell". It is generally known nowadays as "The English Double Daffodil".

This plant, different from the garden plant 'Telamonius Plenus', was (to quote from Wolley-Dod 1890) the double typical wild English daffodil, which occurs wild in Devonshire, in Hampshire, in South Wales, and several other parts of the country. It was the true double form of the wild daffodil rare in cultivation (Backhouse 1912); it was more common than usually supposed, growing freely in Devon, for example (Skelmersdale 1998).

Like 'Telamonius Plenus', it was said to be variable. It too is illustrated in Burbidge (1875) by two blooms, one trumpet-like and one mop-headed; and Burbidge notes that the trumpet form is an accidental occurrence common to all the double-flowered forms of *N. pseudonarcissus*, the species itself being very variable.

As well as 'Telamonius Plenus' and "The English Double Daffodil", Barr eventually noted seven other double forms of *N. pseudonarcissus* in his catalogues. By 1884, for example, he had two more for sale that he identified with those in Parkinson 1629: Pseudonarcissus aureus maximus flore pleno, or "John Tradescant His Great Rose Daffodill" (3), and Pseudonarcissus Gallicus minor flore pleno, or what came to be known as 'Capax Plenus' or 'Eystettensis' or "Queen Anne's Double Daffodil" (4). He listed but did not sell (perhaps he had not even identified or collected them) Parkinson's Pseudonarcissus aureus Hispanicus flore pleno, or "Parkinson's Daffodil" (5), together with Pseudonarcissus Gallicus major flore pleno, or "The Greater Double French Bastard Daffodil" (6). Non-Parkinson daffodils were 'Lobularis Plenus', or "The Dwarf Double Light Yellow" (7) and

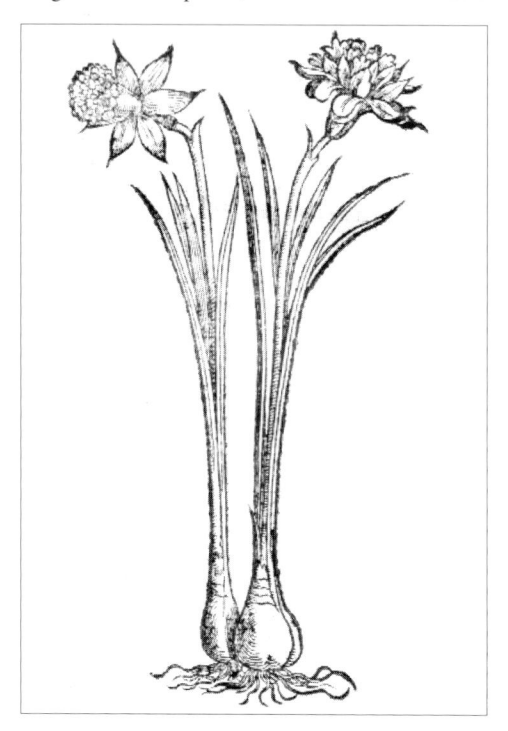

Published in 1605 in Stirpium adversaria nova, *a drawing by Mathias de l'Obel of a double trumpet daffodil found by Gerard in Wiltshire shows a trumpet-like flower and a mop-headed flower produced from the same bulb. Circumstantial evidence suggests that it is "The English Double Daffodil".*

'Lobularis Grandiplenus' (**8**) (both for sale) and 'Nanus Plenus' (**9**) (not for sale). 'Nanus Plenus' later appears with the synonym 'Rip van Winkle'.

Barr thereby covered all of Parkinson's names for double forms of *N. pseudonarcissus* (**1-6**) and added three others (**7-9**).

Parkinson is used as a benchmark on an assumption (that Barr seems to have shared) that Parkinson accounted for all the daffodils which were growing in gardens in England in his time. Writers Clusius, de l'Obel, Besler and Bauhin before him and Morison and Miller after him seem to describe no other varieties, though they might give them different names. That they were the sum of varieties grown in Britain up until Barr's time in the 19c is supposed from the fact that, apart from an influx of Dutch selections from *N. tazetta*, no new introductions of significance were made until Barr's contemporaries Herbert, Leeds and Backhouse began hybridizing.

Barr is used to represent modern times because double yellow trumpets introduced since he was listing them are readily distinguished. They include the old double known as "Thomas' Virescent Daffodil" or "The Derwydd Daffodil" that T H Thomas brought to light in 1888.

Table 1 uses Parkinson's descriptions of numbers **1-6** and Barr's of numbers **7-9** to draw up differences between these daffodils which seem to have been the original double varieties of *N. pseudonarcissus*. Some details on bulb, leaf and stem are given by Parkinson as well as those on flower shape and colouring, but they are omitted here both because of space and because, following the Gibside story, the daffodils among which similarities might be found with the originals were largely identified by flower only.

Table 1 shows that **1** and **2** are very much alike and are variably trumpet-like and mop-headed. A difference between them is that **2** is tinged green beneath some segments.

Numbers **3-9** are always mop-headed. Differences between **1-2** in their mop-headed form and **3-9** are that **3** has a fatter bud with a longer point and has smaller and shorter segments and many more of them; **4** and **6** are self-coloured; **5** has the outer segments curled back and the inner segments sometimes tubular; **7-9** are dwarf and probably have smaller flowers.

A difference between **4** and **6** is that **6** has the segments far less regularly arranged. Of the three dwarf-growing flowers **7-9**, **8** is distinguished by having several centres; while a difference between the other two, **7** and **9**, is that **7** is lighter coloured.

On these comparisons (summarised in Table 2), and always assuming that they are based on valid distinctions, the double daffodil discovered at Gibside resembled **1** or **2**. And as most of the other daffodils reported to the RHS as a result of its discovery were recorded because they looked much the same, so they too resemble **1** or **2**. In order to try and sort them between **1** and **2**, and indeed sift them again in case any did after all resemble any others in the Parkinson/Barr group, 135 reports were selected from the total of 199. These were the reports of daffodils which seemed to have been on site since before 1950. Then, as a few were reports of more than one sort of double on one site, or of doubles at more than one sort of site in the same area, or of more than one sort of double at more than one sort of site in the same area, the number of actual samples rose to 150.

Table 3 shows that two samples did indeed resemble plants other than **1** or **2**, and that on the single criterion of green or no green, thirty-four of the rest resembled **1** (including one query), eighty-one resembled **2** (including one query), one which was yellow in one half of the flower and heavily tinged green in the other half was taken to resemble **1** in one half and **2** in the other, and thirty-two were **1** or **2** but were lacking in enough evidence to say which. Table 3 also shows the different sorts of site that they came from.

Thus on the single character of comparative greenness as mentioned by Parkinson,

39

reports of both 'Telamonius Plenus' (**1**) and "The English Double Daffodil" (**2**) seem to have resulted from the Gibside story. And the reports suggest (though they are a very small sample) that "The English Double Daffodil" is more common than 'Telamonius Plenus'. The enquiry should ideally be widened, however. Comparisons on other characters could confirm or deny the greenness test. For example, it would be interesting to see whether the number of samples resembling each of **1** or **2** would be the same when compared for stem height or bulb size as when compared for greenness. Parkinson says that 'Telamonius Plenus' (**1**) is two foot tall whereas "The English Double Daffodil" (**2**) is only one foot; and that 'Telamonius Plenus' has a thick and great bulb while the bulb of "The English Double Daffodil" is small. Those who put in the reports could be recruited to help with studies based on more than the one character; they could also watch over variability within stocks, for example in height, or incidence of trumpet-like and mop-headed flowers, or timing of appearance of greenness. In addition, more information could be obtained on the daffodils labelled **1** or **2** in Table 3, so that they too might be more nearly identified.

The Gibside story has certainly opened a window onto double trumpet daffodils of a certain age. It has revealed the variations among them and seems to have demonstrated that others besides 'Telamonius Plenus' are among those that have survived.

List of references on request, also a table of comparisons that includes bulb, leaf and stem.

Note that the article does not conclude that all doubles with green patches are "The English Double Daffodil". It mentions double trumpets; of those it takes a group of eight that were described by Parkinson or Barr or both; of those eight it takes two which are different from the other six; it uses the greenness to differentiate between those two and those two only.

The article does not say that other double trumpet doubles do not have green patches (for whatever reason, in whatever circumstances). It says that by a process of elimination it is possible, following Parkinson and Barr, to arrive at two particular double trumpets which closely resemble one another. To distinguish between them as Parkinson did, one can use the characteristic of greenness.

The National Daffodil Society of New Zealand

is the second oldest National Society in the world.
The Society produces three publications each year and is always ready to welcome as members daffodil enthusiasts from anywhere in the world. Keep up with what is happening 'down under' by becoming a member.

Details can be obtained by contacting the
SECRETARY, WILF HALL, 105 WALLACE LOOP ROAD, IHAKARA R.D.1, LEVIN 5500, NEW ZEALAND

VINTAGE DOUBLES

Table 1 Descriptions by Parkinson and Barr of the form and colouring of double trumpet daffodils

	Flower form	**Flower colouring**
(1) "Mr Wilmers Great Double Daffodill" later 'Telamonius Plenus'	Sometimes open, with segments scattered and spread; sometimes with the outer segments separate, and the corona whole and unbroken and filled with segments; sometimes with the corona only half broken.	Whorls of paler and deeper yellow segments intermixed; both yellows ageing to deeper tones.
(2) "Gerrards Double Daffodill" later "The English Double Daffodil"	Like (1) in having the corona variably spreading or closed	Outer whorl of segments the same pale colour as in *N. pseudonarcissus*, inner whorls of segments some pale like the outer, some as deep a yellow as the corona of *N. pseudonarcissus*, some segments with green stripes beneath
(3) "John Tradescant His Great Rose Daffodill"	Bud shorter and thicker and with a longer and sharper point than other daffodils; fl. fully spread open; the segments in whorls one under another, smaller and shorter than in (1), more numerous, "thicker and rounder set together"	Yellow segments and pale segments intermixed
(4) 'Capax Plenus' ('Eystettensis' or "Queen Anne's Double Daffodil")	Two-thirds the size of (6); six whorls of segments, opposite each other and diminishing in size towards centre; no corona	Pale or lemon yellow
(5) "Parkinson's Daffodill"	Always spread open; the outer whorl of segments with apex slightly curled back; the centre whorls smaller and sometimes "hollow trunked"	Outer whorl of segments opening greenish, becoming more yellow; some inner whorls pale yellow, some more gold yellow; greenish, whitish, yellow and gold yellow segments all intermingled
(6) "The Greater Double French Bastard Daffodill"	Buds frequently not opening; fl. half as large again as (4); with more segments more confusedly arranged; the outer whorl tinged green beneath, with apex curled back	Pale whitish yellow or lemon, like (4)
(7) 'Lobularis Plenus' or "The Dwarf Double Light Yellow"	[Dwarf-growing, so fl. may be small]	Light yellow
(8) 'Lobularis Grandiplenus' or "The Dwarf Double Light Yellow With Many Centres"	[Dwarf-growing, so fl. may be small] Fl. broad and spread open; often with 10 or 12 centres, as if several small fls were bound together	Light yellow
(9) 'Nanus Plenus' later 'Rip van Winkle'	[Name Nanus means dwarf, so fl. may be small; identification with 'Rip van Winkle' denotes flower spread open]	Yellow

Table 2 Summary of the differences shown between the daffodils in Table 1

Differences	Daffodil number
mop-head, dwarf and probably small-flowered	(7) (8) (9)
with several centres to the corona	(8)
with one centre to the corona	(7) (9)
yellow	(9)
lighter yellow	(7)
mop-head, self-coloured	(4) (6)
segments regularly arranged	(4)
segments more confusedly arranged	(6)
mop-head, outer segments curled back, inner segments tubular	(5)
mop-head, fat bud with long point, small short and numerous segments	(3)
variably mop-head or trumpet, not resembling any of the above	(1) (2)
tinged green beneath some segments	(2)
no green on segments	(1)

Table 3 Sites of daffodils reported to the RHS in the wake of the Gibside story
Resemblances according to Table 2; resemblances to (1) and (2) therefore measured on the single character of greenness

Site	Resembling (1) "Mr Wilmers Great Double Daffodill"	Resembling (2) "Gerrards Double Daffodill"	Resembling (1) or (2)	Resembling (1) in one half and (2) in the other half	Resembling (8) 'Lobularis Grandiplenus'	Resembling (9) 'Nanus Plenus'
Old garden	18	29	15		1	
Old orchard	6	15	7			
Former grounds of old property	3	7	4			
Estate/former estate/parkland		1	2	1		
Farm/former farm	2	5				
Former nursery		2				
Churchyard	2	5	1			
Former monastic site		2				
Farmland/former farmland	1	7	2			
Woods/commons		3	1			
Uncultivated/formerly uncultivated land	2	5				1
Number of sites	34	81	32	1	1	1

Growing Healthier Daffodils: the Bulb Handling Phase

Gordon Hanks

How flower-bulbs are handled and grown has a great impact on the control (or management) of pests and diseases. What can be termed "physical" methods (how the bulbs are handled) and "cultural" methods (how the plants are grown) have at least an equal place with chemical methods. The aim of this article* is to draw attention to these physical and cultural aspects, and to show how these can be integrated with the effective and safe use of pesticides where these give better (or sometimes the only) means of pest and disease control. Unfortunately, biological methods are not yet established in daffodil growing. This article describes the handling of the dried and cleaned bulbs up to planting time, and a later article will describe operations in the field.

Bulb supply and storage are important factors. As the desiccated "wool" stage of stem nematode can remain active for 25 years, storage and handling areas and bulb equipment should be cleaned and disinfected before use. Dust and debris can also harbour fungal spores and bulb-scale mites. Most bulb growers use formalin as the disinfectant, but newer materials are now being recommended. Where hot-water treatment (HWT) facilities are available and trays or other containers are to be used, they can be sterilised by immersion at 50°C (122°F) for ten minutes with a disinfectant.

An ideal general storage temperature is 17°C (63°F), which is too low for basal rot development and warm enough to prevent retardation of the buds within. Ensuring adequate air movement round the bulbs, either naturally or by fans, is equally important, preventing sweating, the spread of moulds, and premature rooting. Bins of bulbs can still be seen parked in the sun in yards! High temperatures and humidities can rapidly result in bulbs being reduced to a musty mass by the fungus *Rhizopus*. Poor bulbs in poor conditions attract pests such as the small narcissus flies and bulb mites, which do not attack healthy bulbs.

Hot-water treatment is critical, time-consuming, messy, expensive... and unavoidable! As well as your own planting stock, any bulbs being brought onto the premises should be inspected carefully, and should be given HWT, particularly to avoid introducing stem nematodes. Stem nematode nowadays appears to be more prevalent amongst United Kingdom daffodils, and apparent freedom from nematode symptoms is no justification to avoid HWT, since very few nematodes can kill a bulb in a year. HWT with formalin was designed to combat stem nematode, but is also more than enough to kill fungal spores and pests like bulb-scale mite and the larvae of the large narcissus fly.

To reduce damage, HWT should normally be done after the flower bud initials have been fully formed (when the trumpet or cup initial is visible with a hand-lens after dissecting the flower bud), and before there is too much activity of the root initials. This means HWT is carried out in late-July or early-August in the United Kingdom, there being a safe working "window" of about four weeks. The standard United Kingdom recommendation is to use a treatment of three hours at 44.4°C (111.9°F) with formalin and a non-ionic wetter. Assuming the temperature of the HWT tank falls a little after the start of immersion, the three hours should be timed from when the 44.4°C is restored. This temperature is critical, and although the preciseness of "44.4°C" often amuses non-bulb growers, many experts consider that modern equipment should be able to maintain temperature control to within plus or minus 0.1°C. We know that 43°C (109.4°F) is inadequate for controlling stem nematodes, 47°C (116.6°F) can cause a reduction in growth, and 50°C (122°F), even for a short time, can be lethal to bulbs.

A disinfectant - traditionally commercial formalin diluted 1:200 with water - is usually considered essential, though other disinfectants are being used and there are data showing that longer HWT times may circumvent the need to include the formalin. This should not be tried until recommendations have been developed in the United Kingdom! This formalin concentration should be adhered to, for too low a rate is ineffective, and too high a rate can damage the base plate and roots. It is common to add a fungicide to the HWT tank to control *Fusarium* rots, an insecticide is sometimes added to prevent subsequent infection by large narcissus fly, and an "anti-foam" preparation should be used where the tank set-up leads to foaming as nematodes may survive on the cooler foam. When topping up tanks, chemicals should be used at the original rate, unless the manufacturer's instructions advise differently.

Damage caused by HWT means that bulbs intended for forcing should not receive the treatment, and commercial growers "sterilise" only their replanting stocks. HWT can cause minor but tolerable damage even when carried out correctly. HWT applied too early, too late, for too long, at too high a temperature, or with the wrong chemicals and concentrations, causes a spectrum of symptoms from a mild mottling of the leaf tips, through malformed flowers, to widespread root and leaf loss. Where good flowers are needed in the year following HWT, other temperature treatments are available to mitigate HWT damage. The simplest technique is to store bulbs at 18°C (64°F) for two weeks before HWT. The standard method in Cornwall involves "pre-warming" bulbs for one week at 30°C (86°F), though three to seven days at 30-35°C (86-95°F) seems to be acceptable. After this the bulbs are "pre-soaked" in non-heated water with the usual formalin for at least three hours (overnight is acceptable), and then HWT is carried out at 46°C (114.8°F). These warm storage treatments appear to retard growth temporarily, rendering the new organs less sensitive to high temperatures.

Daffodil bulbs with stem nematode symptoms should be lifted and hot-water treated early. Before HWT, they should not be warm-stored or allowed to dry out, both of which increase and spread the infestation. It is vital to segregate these bulbs from your main stock. Early HWT is also more effective in controlling base rot, and in both these instances a measure of damage from HWT has to be endured.

The **choice of site** for growing daffodils is often beyond control. However warm sites such as those which are very sheltered or on a south-facing slope will encourage base rot (*Fusarium* rots). Similarly nearby shelter may provide a warmer habitat for the large narcissus fly, and the presence of other daffodils close-by may form a reserve of pests and diseases. Daffodils are grown successfully on many soil types, but soil should be free-draining and not compacted, as standing water will spread stem nematode. Good crop rotation is an important aspect of **site preparation**, and helps reduce weed, pest and disease problems and rids the soil of daffodils left behind during lifting, as well as maintaining soil structure. A six- to eight-year break is considered ideal for daffodils, as *Fusarium* spores can be long-lived. Two types of preceding crops should be avoided: first, those leaving a high residue (e.g. brassicas) which increases nitrogen supply, leading to readier infection with the base rot fungus, and, secondly, crops that can host stem nematode. The latter include other bulbs, legumes, root crops, sweet corn, strawberries and many common weeds.

* *This article is a summary of a detailed paper, which can be obtained free from the office at Horticulture Research International, Kirton, Lincs PE20 1NN, UK (telephone +44 (0) 1205 723477, fax +44 (0) 1205 724957, or email Gordon.Hanks@hri.ac.uk.*

My Work With the Genus Narcissus

Frank B Galyon

My love for daffodils goes back a long way. At age four I was allotted my own garden space at my combined parents' and grandparents' home. The first thing I planted in it was a very early yellow trumpet daffodil known to the family as the "Woodruff" daffodil as it came from the Woodruff's home place. It bloomed before *N. pseudonarcissus* and its flowers were better. When we moved to our present location I still had a bulb of this daffodil. One of the early crosses I made was that of *N. obvallaris* × "Woodruff". I still have a few clones that resulted from this cross. Through the years I have attempted to identify the "Woodruff" daffodil. Of the diploid yellow trumpets, I have grown both 'Golden Spur' and 'Ard Righ' and it is neither one of those. I have seen neither 'Henry Irving' nor 'M. J. Berkeley', but based on the photograph of 'Henry Irving' in *Daffodil Growing for Pleasure and Profit* by A F Calvert (London 1929) I have concluded that the "Woodruff" daffodil was actually 'Henry Irving'.

Pollen

In breeding daffodils I attribute great importance to the collection of pollen. I always try to collect the stamens the first thing in the morning before the anthers of the opening flowers have dehisced. This serves two purposes: first, it allows one to acquire all the pollen from the flower; second, by getting the stamens out of the flower before any pollen grains emerge, one is completely sure that no self-pollination of that flower has taken place. I then place the undehisced anthers in small sliding cardboard pillboxes; leaving them half open so that air reaches the anthers. After twenty-four hours the anthers will have shed their pollen grains so that one may use them for pollination. The pollen boxes are left at room temperature for seven days. At the end of that time I place the loaded pollen boxes directly into the freezing unit of the refrigerator. It is not necessary to use either silica gel or any other drying agent. The freezing unit alone keeps the pollen viable for at least three years. My "pollen bank" of frozen pollen allows me to make crosses between cultivars that bloom at different times. Whenever I use frozen pollen I immediately return it to the freezer after its use. It has been my observation that pollen older than three years lacks viability. Therefore I discard the frozen pollen after three years. I prefer to use fresh pollen whenever available, but when it is not I don't hesitate to use pollen from my pollen bank. I have had good success using frozen pollen.

Early days

My first successful daffodil pollination occurred in 1974. Bill Pannill was most generous in letting me have pollen from his flowers that were better than those I was growing. That year I harvested 1,375 seeds from 138 seedpods. Not knowing that daffodil seeds are doubly dormant, requiring a warm moist period before a cold moist period, I didn't get around to planting my seeds until 5 January 1975. As a result of late planting my 1974 seeds didn't germinate until 1976. In the summer of 1977 I transplanted my two-year-old seedlings into rows in the field. In 1980 I had the first blooms on my own seedlings. There were blooms on two siblings from the cross of 'Silver Bells' ×

'Quick Step'. One of the two had good pollen which I used on its sibling, resulting in two seed…more on that later.

Raising early flowering daffodils

A major appeal to me of daffodils is the fact that they are among the earliest of flowers to bloom and I always enjoy the winter gold that they provide. With that in mind I requested pollens from early-flowering cultivars from Rosewarne EHS in Cornwall, as I knew they were working to get earlier and earlier blooms. Barbara Fry first sent me pollens in 1977. That was the year that I learned of the existence of the cultivar 'Rijnveld's Early Sensation' ('RES') and began using it to obtain early-flowering seedlings on my own. As soon as 'Dawn Chorus' became available I acquired a bulb. Its parentage is 'RES' crossed with an autumn flowering *N. asturiensis*. 'Dawn Chorus' usually blooms a few days before 'RES'. I soon made the cross of 'RES' × 'Dawn Chorus' and I still grow a couple of siblings from that cross that are superior to both parents. Right away I put 'RES' pollen onto the earlier flowering 2Y-Rs that I had, in an effort to put the red-orange colouring onto earlier flowers. I soon discovered that it takes two generations to accomplish that result. One of the better crosses made along these lines was the cross of 'Monal' × 'RES'. The earliest blooming seedling from this cross was backcrossed onto 'Monal'. In this second generation cross the red-orange colour occurred on an earlier-flowering plant.

A second interest of mine has been double daffodils. Most of the doubles are late bloomers and fail to open properly in my climate in Tennessee. In an effort to get earlier blooming doubles I crossed 'Oregon Beauty' × 'Dawn Chorus'. I have some very early-flowering doubles from this cross. So far I have not yet bloomed any second-generation seedlings from this line.

Division 5

On one of my early daffodil orders to Grant Mitsch, he very kindly included three bulbs of *N. triandrus* subsp. *triandrus* var. *triandrus* gratis. Most of the first generation hybrids between the species *N. triandrus* and tetraploids daffodils have proved to be sterile. Paradoxically, both 'Silver Bells and 'Honey Bells' were two of the first generation triploid hybrids from *N. triandrus* that proved to be fertile by setting seed. I reasoned that by back-crossing 'Silver Bells' with pollen of the species *N. triandrus* one might obtain seedlings which looked more like the species and which might also be fertile. This has proved to be the case, for I recently flowered a small 5W-W from the cross of 'Silver Bells' × *N. triandrus* subsp. *triandrus* var. *triandrus*. This seedling did prove to be fertile when its pollen was backcrossed to the species *N. triandrus*, but it failed to set seed to its own pollen. When 'Honey Bells' was crossed by pollen of *N. triandrus* I grew eight seedlings. 'Honey Bells' had a weak bulb that often succumbed to basal rot. Most of my eight seedlings from 'Honey Bells' × *N. triandrus* were interfertile but eventually I lost all of these first generation backcrosses. Before losing them I obtained five second-generation hybrids by sibling-crossing the first generation hybrids. One of the second-generation hybrids is larger and more robust. It has fertility in both directions and I suspect that it may be a tetraploid 5Y-Y. It has been admired in my garden and if it proves amenable to culture it may ultimately be named and introduced. It is my belief that the clone 'Honey Bells' is no longer in existence anywhere in the world. All bulbs that I have recently obtained as 'Honey Bells' have turned out to be 'Harmony Bells' instead. 'Honey Bells' had a normal style that was easy to pollinate. On the other hand 'Harmony Bells' has a style that is recessed below the stamens. In order to pollinate it is necessary tear down the flower structure to show the stigma on the extremely recessed style. For this reason there should be no confusion between these two somewhat similar cultivars. Ron Scamp's lovely 5Y-Y 'Cariad' is fertile both ways. 'Cariad' has unfortunately been in limited supply ever since its introduction. When it becomes more readily available I feel sure that it will make a sizeable impact in producing lovely fertile triandrus hybrids. 'Mission Bells' has recently been counted as a tetraploid 5W-W. Nevertheless it seems less fertile as a seed parent than its parent, the triploid 'Silver Bells'. Just this year I obtained two apparently normal seeds from the cross of 'Akepa' × 'Cariad'.

Division 6
Cyclamineus hybrids have always appealed to me. Their jaunty reflexed perianths combined with their earliness of flowering are a natural combination of my tastes in daffodils. I have pursued backcrossing the first generation cyclamineus hybrids by using pollen of the species *N. cyclamineus*. Some especially attractive flowers have come from the cross of 'Surfside' × *N. cyclamineus*. Other similar crosses have been made.

Extending the division 7 break-through
Hybrids obtained by crossing *N. jonquilla* onto standard daffodils grow and bloom especially well in Tennessee. The fertile jonquil hybrid 'Quick Step' opened the possibility of breeding fertile jonquil hybrids. Next came along the fertile 'Hillstar'. The fertile 'Limequilla' followed this. These three fertile amphidiploids are yielding ever more interesting seedlings when crossed together. Some of the more interesting ones in my seedling patch have come from crossing 'Limequilla' with 'Hillstar'. It is of interest that 'Quick Step' carries only a single dose of the W-gene that causes whiteness in daffodils. 'Hillstar' carries only one dose of the L-gene for lemon coloured perianths. 'Hillstar' when self-pollinated yields a fair proportion of deep gold selfs as a result of segregating out this L-gene in the next generation. Likewise, 'Limequilla' carries only a single dose of the dominant gene for pale colouring. The serendipitous occurrence of unreduced gametes from the diploid *N. jonquilla* that resulted in 'Quick Step', 'Hillstar' and 'Limequilla' has opened up what will be a floodgate of fertile jonquil hybrids in the future. From the writings of Dr Fernandez it was known that a tetraploid form of *N. fernandesii* existed. Likewise he had mentioned that a tetraploid form of *N. jonquilla* also existed. If one could acquire these tetraploid forms, one could use their pollen on standard tetraploid daffodils, resulting in instant fertile amphidiploid seedlings of various colour combinations. Eventually I tracked down both of the tetraploid forms of these species. Michael Salmon of Monocot Nurseries was able to furnish me with a bulb of the tetraploid *N. fernandesii* var. *major* and the tetraploid form of *N. jonquilla*. For the first time in the 2000 season I flowered seedlings that resulted from crossing the tetraploid *N. jonquilla* and standard daffodils. One of these seedlings was from a cross 'Quasar' × 'Magician' with tetraploid *N. jonquilla*. On maiden bloom this seedling surpassed anything I had seen among fertile 7W-Ps. Its pollen proved to be as fertile as any of the fertile jonquil hybrids, thus proving the usefulness of new jonquil hybrids that result from using the tetraploid form of *N. jonquilla*. Manuel Lima kindly sent me pollen from two of his first generation hybrids of *N. viridiflorus*. These were 'El Camino' × *N. viridiflorus* and 'Actaea' × *N. viridiflorus*. This pollen was used on four fertile jonquil hybrids. In 2001 I had blooms on a seedling from the cross of 'Hillstar' × ('El Camino' × *N. viridiflorus*). It showed its heritage by earliness of bloom, tallness of stem, and by its greenish-lemon perianth. John Hunter of New Zealand has already named a first-generation hybrid of *N. viridiflorus* 'Emerald Sea'. *N. viridiflorus* itself is not winter-hardy in my climate. I suspect that that may also be the case with its first generation hybrids. When I first learned of the existence of 'Emerald Sea', I asked John Hunter to pollinate 'Limequilla' and 'Emerald Sea' for me and then send me the seed. He very kindly did this, and now I have seventeen three-year old seedlings from this cross planted out in my field. John will of course bloom his own seedlings from this cross long before I do. Crosses of this sort

will greatly expand the gene pool of fertile jonquil hybrids both as to colour, season of bloom, and number of florets per stem.

More hybridizing results

Earlier I mentioned obtaining seeds from crossing together two siblings of 'Silver Bells' × 'Quick Step'. Diploid forms of NJ, NTr and JTr are routinely sterile eg 'Hawera'. It is thus rather surprising that forms having the same makeup of NNJTr show some fertility. The only possible explanation for this is that meiosis does somehow occur, resulting in fertile gametes. The cross of 'Ice Chimes' × 'Hillstar' has also yielded seedlings with some fertility.

Last year I succeeded in effecting the cross of the 35 chromosome 'White Owl' × 'Matador'. I have found that tazetta seedlings are extremely slow in growing to flowering size here in Tennessee. For that reason I sent these seeds to a friend in California to grow in his climate, which is much more amenable to raising tazetta hybrids from seed.

Another interest of mine has been in the very late flowering daffodils. An object of mine was to introduce more colour into the late bloomers. I ceased making crosses among my late flowering Y-R seedlings after blooming Brian Duncan's 'Burning Bush' for the first time. Here 'Burning Bush' blooms with the poets and is everything one could desire in a very late Y-R. I have had a little more success with getting better 3W-Rs by using 'Lisbarnett' with other very late cultivars. I continue to make poeticus crosses and have obtained a few very attractive 9W-Rs by using 'Felindre' as a parent in both directions.

Dick and Elise Havens have been kind enough to grow on several of my selected seedlings to see if they merit later introduction. In 1999 they introduced my first named cultivar to the trade. It is named 'Millie Galyon' 2W-R after my wife. Its origin was 'Dewy Rose' × 'Pipestone'. It had won the Grant and Amy Mitsch Award at the ADS convention in Jackson, Mississippi. A few improved 2W-Ps and 2W-Rs are showing up among the seedlings from the red-pink 'Millie Galyon'.

It has been a great deal of fun working with species daffodils. Just this season I germinated three seedlings from the cross of *N. hedraeanthus* × 'Straight Arrow'. Who knows what that cross will yield? It is just a matter of waiting to see. I have had some success with miniatures. My cross of 'Inca' × *N. cyclamineus* yielded a quite lovely small thing with lemon reflexed perianth and corona that reverses completely to white. This seedling has set seed with *N. cyclamineus* pollen, which should yield some 6Y-W seedlings that should be even smaller. Another interesting seedling was obtained by crossing 'Mite' using pollen of 'Snipe'. The best seedling from this progeny is quite small and opens 6W-Y only to fade eventually to 6W-W. Its pollen is extremely fertile, but so far it has failed as a seed parent.

I continue to make crosses among the standard daffodils in the first four divisions yet I must confess that my greater interest lies in divisions five, six and seven. My keenest interest in the genus *Narcissus* has to be simply the making of pollinations, raising seedlings to first flowering and going on from there. It invariably occurs that I get over-enthusiastic in making crosses. This year I planted over 2,000 seeds here in Knoxville – far too many! In addition I sent seeds to California, Ohio, Minnesota, Oregon and as far away as New Zealand. Also I have enjoyed sending excess pollen to those people requesting it when it is available.

The fertility of triploid daffodils

Finally I feel that some statement about the fertility of triploid daffodils must be made. E K Janaki Ammal stated, "we have in the triploid daffodil the point of origin of a great many beautiful forms. What is it that makes the triploid so unique…the unbalanced chromosome number results in the production of occasional tetraploids…as Maximus did in the production of… 'King Alfred'? Also as triploids produce germ cells with chromosome numbers varying from the basic numbers 7 – 14, the progeny from them may thus have one or more chromosomes more or less than the usual set...it is through and from triploids that these irregularities (aneuploids) originate. So I say to all daffodil breeders, look to your triploids and you can still get greater surprises."

A J Bateman stated, "Triploid plants have each of the normal set of chromosomes represented three times...the three representatives of each type of chromosome cannot be divided equally into two. At maturation division for the germ cells...sometimes the daughter cell will have all or nearly all chromosomes represented once, or all or nearly all represented twice, and then will be viable."

Peter E Brandham stated "The three sets of chromosomes in the triploids form threes (trivalents) at meiosis which segregate irregularly to give gametes with a wide range of chromosome numbers...in general, triploids have low fertility and...any progeny that they do produce is just as likely to be diploid or tetraploid as it is to be triploid."

I have to disagree with Dr Brandham who implies that triploid daffodils are of low fertility. It has been my experience that triploid daffodils of the NNN type are quite fertile both as seed parents and pollen parents. Their fertility is not dependent on the formation of unreduced gametes. Among the triploid daffodil cultivars of the NNN type that are fertile are the following; 'Dinkie', 'Emperor', 'Empress', 'Magnificence', 'Maximus', 'Minuet' and *Poeticus recurvus*. It is of interest that both diploids and tetraploids have been counted among the progeny of these fertile triploids. This fact leads one to believe that meiosis of these triploids takes place in some fashion to yield both haploid and diploid gametes leading in the next generation to diploid, triploid or tetraploid clones. While not all triploid cyclamineus hybrids are fertile, numbers of CNN triploid clones are fertile. There is also the previously-mentioned case of fertility of a few triploid triandrus hybrids. One of the earliest instances of the formation of a tetraploid daffodil, 'King Alfred', occurred as a result of the mating of the two triploid daffodils, 'Maximus' and 'Emperor'. [See Peter Brandham's article on page 50]

Possible later introduction

A few of my own seedlings that are being grown on for possible later introduction are the following:

1. An early 2Y-Y from 'Monal' × 'RES'
2. An early 2O-R from 'Sabine Hay' × 'Monal'
3. A 5W-W from the cross 'Silver Bells' x 'Quick Step'
4. A 2Y-R from the cross of 'Glenfarclas' × ('Monal × 'RES')
5. An excellent 6Y-W from the cross of 'Inca' × *N. cyclamineus*
6. A 6W-Y with great contrast from the cross of an unknown 1W-Y × *N. cyclamineus*
7. A miniature 6Y-Y from the cross 'Little Gem' × *N. cyclamineus*
8. A 5Y-Y from the cross of two siblings from the cross 'Honey Bells' × *N. triandrus* subsp. *triandrus* var. *triandrus*
9. A 5Y-Y from the cross *N. fernandesii* × *N. triandrus triandrus*
10. A paler 5Y-Y from the cross *N. triandrus* subsp. *triandrus* var. *triandrus* × *N. jonquilla*

Bibliography:

Calvert, A F "Daffodil Crosses" p94 in *RHS Daffodil Yearbook 1936*.
Coleman, C J "Ancestors" p7 in *RHS Daffodil Yearbook 1939*.
Janaki Ammal, E K "Chromosomes and the Daffodil Breeder" p31 in *RHS Daffodil Yearbook 1949*.
Bateman, A J "The Genetics of Narcissus" p28 in *RHS Daffodil Yearbook 1954*.
Brandham, P E "Bigger and Better; the evolution of polyploid Narcissus in cultivation" p57 in *RHS Daffodil Yearbook 1986*.
Galyon, F B "The Terminology of Daffodil Breeding" p18 in *The ADS Daffodil Journal* Vol 33, number 1, Sept 1996.

Triploidy in Narcissus, the Fertility Debate

Peter Brandham

In a number of publications over the past few years I have maintained that triploid *Narcissus* cultivars are highly sterile, basing my conclusions on the predictably irregular sexual behaviour of the chromosomes of these plants. Misinterpreting this statement as meaning *totally* sterile, several correspondents and plant breeders have rightly pointed out that they have obtained viable seed from a cross involving such-and-such triploid cultivar and that I must therefore be wrong in my conclusions.

In this article I shall outline the mechanism causing the sterility of these plants and will show how everyone can be right in this debate, but first I must explain the process of normal, fertile reproduction that occurs in non-triploids.

Life cycles, meiosis and non-reduction

Fertility in all sexually-reproducing plants and animals depends on the accurate functioning of the following life cycle, which is abbreviated in different ways in some groups of living organisms: -

Fusion of the cell contents, and especially the nuclei, of specialised male and female sex cells or gametes to produce a zygote, in which the chromosome number is doubled: Growth A, of the zygote: Meiosis in some cells which halves the chromosome number again: Growth B, of the meiotic product: Formation of gametes capable of sexual fusion, as above, to complete the cycle.

In most plants, two periods of vegetative or mitotic growth incorporating stability of chromosome number occur in this cycle, A growth and B growth. Their relative importance and extent depend on the degree of evolutionary advancement of the species in question. In some algae such as *Spirogyra* and desmids there is no A growth, the products of gamete fusion passing directly into meiosis. In other algae such as most brown seaweeds and in most sexually-reproducing animals the reverse applies, with A growth only and no B growth. Meiosis in these gives rise immediately to gametes. Mosses and liverworts have some A growth, but more B growth, i.e. after meiosis. All higher plants have a little B growth but much more A growth, after gamete fusion.

In diploid *Narcissus*, in common with all other diploid higher plants and most animals, including humans, there are two matching or homologous sets of chromosomes in every individual. Each set is inherited from one of the individual's parents and carries a full complement of genes. Meiosis occurs in the developing sex cells, i.e. in flowering plants in the pollen mother cells of the anthers on the male side of the flower and in the single embryo mother cell in each ovule on the female side. It halves the chromosome number to produce the haploid cells that will give rise to the gametes after a very limited amount of B growth. It involves the accurate pairing of the sets of chromosomes contributed to the plant by each of its parents, i.e. chromosome no. 1 of one set pairs with no. 1 from the other, no. 2 pairs with no. 2 etc. There are seven such pairs, making 14 chromosomes, in most *Narcissus* species, but ten or eleven pairs in *N. tazetta* and its allies. When paired as bivalents the chromosomes exchange genetic material, effectively re-shuffling the genes contributed to the individual by its parents. They then separate and later divide synchronously to form haploid cells, each with a single set of chromosomes, that will produce gametes after B growth of no more than three further doublings.

In a single cell of a diploid *Narcissus* that is going through meiosis, the pairing and separation of the two chromosomes in every one of the seven bivalents must be completely accurate and synchronised in order to ensure the viability of the gametes produced from that cell. In most diploid species and cultivars this is so, but if only one pair of chromosomes fails to associate in a meiotic cell, or if only one bivalent fails to separate properly, the gametes resulting from that cell will have one chromosome missing or one that is duplicated. This chromosomal imbalance causes the abortion of the gametes and lowers the fertility of the plant. Evidence of the non-production or the loss of these aneuploid gametes is provided by the fact that no diploid *Narcissus* cultivar has yet been reported to have 13 or 15 chromosomes. All have the regular 14, except those with *tazetta* ancestry.

One abnormality associated with meiosis is the production of non-reduced gametes, an event that is quite rare but that has been of major importance in the evolution of *Narcissus* cultivars. In this process, a diploid cell that is due to halve its chromosome number via meiosis avoids it and produces one or more gametes (after some B growth) with the same diploid chromosome number as that of the parent plant. These non-reduced gametes have two full sets of chromosomes instead of one, but there is no imbalance and they are viable. After pollination, each will fuse with a normal haploid gamete from another diploid parent to produce a triploid seed with (in the case of most *Narcissus*) three sets of seven, or 21 chromosomes.

Triploidy

Triploids are often much more vigorous and showy than their diploid relatives. They are therefore frequently selected as good cultivars, but they are largely sterile. In *Narcissus*, sterility arising from triploidy is not a major disadvantage, since the cultivars are routinely propagated vegetatively in order that their genetic integrity can be maintained, but it causes problems to the breeder as far as the production of further seed progeny from them is concerned. Triploids are not totally sterile, however. Some retain a small incidence of fertile meiotically-produced gametes, depending on their chromosomal constitution. Additionally, they can all produce small numbers of fertile non-reduced gametes, as described above, but with three sets of chromosomes. When one of the latter unites with a normal haploid gamete with one set, as produced by a normal diploid, it will give rise to a tetraploid seed with four sets of chromosomes. Late in the nineteenth century, this process resulted in the appearance of the first tetraploid *Narcissus* cultivars, which in their turn have produced the host of tetraploids which now comprise the majority of the cultivars of the genus.

Sexually-produced gametes of triploid *Narcissus*, following meiosis, are mostly sterile because of their chromosomal imbalance. Their degree of imbalance and the level of sterility depend on the precise chromosomal constitution of the triploid in question, with one class of triploids, the autotriploids, being more fertile than the other, the allotripoloids.

Autotriploids

Autotriploids are produced within a single species and have three haploid sets of chromosomes that are virtually identical to each other. They have a chance of at least some gamete fertility, the degree of which can be forecast quite accurately as follows:

Let us assume that a full haploid set of chromosomes in a species, with all of the constituent genes that are vital for its existence, comprises just one chromosome, rather than seven as in most *Narcissus* (Note that this is simply an example, since no plant has ever been found with only one chromosome in a haploid set). A triploid will therefore contain three identical chromosomes in each cell. Prior to gamete production, they will associate together during meiosis to form not a bivalent of two chromosomes but a trivalent of three. After exchange of genetic material, the three chromosomes will separate inevitably with one moving one way (say downwards) and two the other (upwards). The products will not comprise all haploid cells, as in diploid meiosis, but equal numbers of haploid cells with a single chromosome and diploid cells with two. They would all be genetically and chromosomally balanced and the plant would be fully fertile, producing equal numbers of haploid and diploid gametes.

Now let us assume that a haploid set comprises two chromosomes, numbered 1 and 2. A triploid would therefore contain six chromosomes in every cell, in three sets of two. Each meiotic cell would form two trivalents (1-1-1 and 2-2-2). In each of these trivalents the unequal 2-1 separation following genetic material exchange will be quite independent of the other. If the first trivalent separates as two chromosomes downwards and one upwards and the second does likewise, the "lower" half of the products will be diploid with two sets of two chromosomes (numbers 1,1,2,2) and the "upper" half will be haploid with one set of two (numbers 1,2), and all would be viable. On the other hand, because of the randomness of their separation, the second trivalent is equally likely to separate the opposite way around, as one downwards and two upwards. The lower meiotic product would then contain three chromosomes, (1,1,2), and the upper would also contain three, (1,2,2), but both would be non-functional because of their genetic imbalance.

Because of the random separation of trivalents, a triploid with three sets of two chromosomes will therefore produce gametes of four different chromosomal constitutions in equal numbers (1,2; 1,1,2,2; 1,1,2 and 1,2,2). Of these, only the first two (or 50 per cent of the total) are viable, chromosomally and genetically balanced, with half of them being diploid and half haploid.

In a triploid with three sets of three chromosomes, the first two bivalents will form the same four types of meiotic product as above (1,2; 1,1,2,2; 1,1,2 and 1,2,2) in equal numbers. To each of these there is an equal probability that the third trivalent, 3-3-3, will add either one or two of its chromosomes. Thus there are eight possible gamete types produced in equal numbers by this individual (1,2,3; 1,2,3,3; 1,1,2,2,3; 1,1,2,2,3,3; 1,1,2,3; 1,1,2,3,3; 1,2,2,3; and 1,2,2,3,3), of which only two are balanced and viable, the haploid 1,2,3 and the diploid 1,1,2,2,3,3. The plant therefore will be only 25 per cent fertile.

Clearly, because of the independent separation of trivalents and the non-survival of gametes with an imbalance of chromosome number, the addition of further chromosomes to the set will halve the incidence of chromosomally balanced viable gametes with each addition. Gametes of an autotriploid with three sets of three are 25 per cent balanced (or euploid) and viable, with three sets of four 12.5 per cent of them would be balanced, three sets of five 6.25 per cent, three sets of six 3.125 per cent and three sets of seven 1.5625 per cent. This last figure is the expected percentage of viable balanced diploid or haploid gametes produced by those autotriploid *Narcissus* cultivars which have three sets of seven chromosomes. In terms of the actual fertility of the plant, this percentage would be slightly higher, since aneuploid gametes with the diploid chromosome number minus one or sometimes even two are sometimes viable enough to effect a fertilisation. This is because their genetic imbalance is not too extreme. An example in *Narcissus* would be one with chromosomes 1,1,2,2,3,3,4,5,5,6,6,7,7 where one of the fourth pair of chromosomes is missing. Haploid chromosome numbers plus one or two do not survive as gametes, as explained above.

Fertility in autotriploids can also be raised further by the unknown but invariably low frequency of viable non-reduced triploid gametes that they are capable of forming. Even with the addition of these to the viable aneuploid gametes mentioned above, the total fertility would not be expected to be much more than double the incidence of viable diploid or haploid gametes, making a maximum of 3-4 per cent overall. In terms of viable ovules in an ovary of *Narcissus*, which normally average 40-50 in a fertile diploid, this figure becomes 1-2 in any single ovary. Following pollination, even by a fully fertile pollen parent, this might not be enough to result in the ripening of the seeds, even if they were potentially viable. On the other hand, if the same cross is done with the male and female roles reversed, 3-4 per cent of the total pollen in an autotriploid anther is still quite a respectable number of good pollen grains. The take-home message, as far as making diploid / autotriploid hybridisations is concerned, is therefore to use the triploid as the pollen parent to optimise the chances of success. The chances of a reasonable number of successful fertilisations can be increased still further if as much pollen as possible is loaded onto the stigma.

Allotriploids

In allotriploids the three sets of chromosomes are not identical, because two or more distinct species feature in their ancestry. In some allotriploids, two sets of chromosomes are the same, with the third set structurally and/or genetically different. Often the difference is extreme, as in triploids derived in part from the *tazetta* alliance, such as 'Jumblie', 'Quince' and 'Tête-à-tête'. These have 7+7+10 or 7+7+11 = 24 or 25 chromosomes. Allotriploid cultivars of this type have a confused meiosis. Their two sets of similar chromosomes pair and separate accurately to produce potentially haploid gametes, but the third set does not pair well with the other two, if at all. Its constituent chromosomes separate roughly into two groups concurrently with bivalent separation, so that every meiotic product has one set of seven chromosomes plus a few odd ones from the set of 10 or 11. The latter create a genetic and chromosomal imbalance and all of the resulting meiotic products are non-viable.

In other allotriploids the three sets of chromosomes are all too dissimilar to pair effectively during meiosis. They form a confused mass in the meiotic cells, with the formation of some bivalents or trivalents, but with the majority of the chromosomes remaining unpaired. Separation is again roughly into two groups, resulting in extreme imbalance and non-viability of the meiotic products.

Thus, unlike the situation in autotriploids, the probability that allotriploids will produce viable haploid or diploid gametes falls practically to zero. Again, the occurrence of non-reduced triploid gametes in these plants will nevertheless give a small amount of fertility.

Conclusion

In view of what I have set out above, is it worth the effort to include any triploids in a breeding programme? The answer is categorically yes, because many of them are vigorous, showy, or have other valuable characteristics. They are all highly sterile, but never totally so. Indeed the only totally sterile *Narcissus* cultivars are those double-flowered varieties (diploid, triploid or otherwise) in which all of the sexual parts of the flower are converted into perianth-like or corona-like structures, resulting in the complete absence of a stigma and/or pollen. Triploid cultivars will always produce some fertile gametes, which can be haploid, diploid or triploid, and there is a possibility of some success in breeding from them, especially if they are used as pollen parents and if more duplicate crosses are done than would be normal otherwise. It is a lost cause to try to cross two triploids together, as their combined low fertilities will prevent any viable progeny from appearing, but if triploids are crossed with fertile diploid or tetraploid partners there is a good chance that at least a few interesting offspring will ensue. Many of these will also be polyploid and will display the associated characteristics of shape, size and vigour that are the goals of so many breeding programmes.

Australia Speaking With One Voice

Tony Davis

For many years the daffodil world in Australia revolved around the Tasmanian Daffodil Council and the Australian Daffodil Society. The latter body was set up by growers in Victoria with the laudable aim of representing all Australian daffodil growers. Tasmania and the other states did not agree with that move and Western Australia and New South Wales/ACT subsequently set up their own associations to co-ordinate their local activities. Consultation between the states was infrequent and not always constructive.

At the World Daffodil Convention in New Zealand in 1984 informal discussions between a numbers of Australian growers resolved to take steps to rectify the obvious problem. The first step was to hold a National Championship in Canberra in 1986 at which attempts would be made to move towards a truly national body. The show was very successful with growers from all states participating. Some progress was also made toward standardizing classes, definitions and the like but it was clear that a National Association was a long way off.

There was a desire to continue to resolve outstanding issues and subsequent national championships saw progress in this regard. The first major achievement was to set up a loose framework for the National Daffodil Association of Australia and the election of an International Liaison officer to provide a central contact point between Australia and international bodies. That position is currently held by Mrs Jennie Jamieson, 11 Bromley Place, Kingsley, Western Australia (Phone 08 9409 1156).

A significant recent change has seen the body representing Victoria change its name to the Victorian Daffodil Society Inc. This should remove much of the confusion overseas bodies have about the structure in Australia.

Much work still needs to be done to get the National Daffodil Association of Australia elevated to the primary position in the country. However, it will happen over time. In the meantime, daffodil enquiries about Australia should be directed through Jennie Jamieson. She will be able to provide a great deal of information about shows, contacts, flower registrations, quarantine requirements and the like.

Major shows for 2002	
Hobart	6-8 September
Launceston	14-15 September
Liongatha (Vic)	5-7 September
Canberra	14-15 September
Perth	5-7 September

The World Convention in 2004 will be held in Melbourne during 11-12 September and pre and post convention tours will be available. Contact Ian Dyson on telephone 03 5978 6005 for more information.

Footnote
The *Yearbook* has always aimed to serve all its international readership. In the case of daffodils many enthusiasts belong to more than one national society and visits to growers and shows overseas are becoming increasingly popular. With this in mind we hope to publish a short article each year giving information about how to access daffodil enthusiasts and shows in particular countries. [Editor]

The Floriade

Jan Pennings

This world flower exhibition is held every ten years in Holland, under the auspices of the AIPH. It is the shop-window where we show to people from all over the world what we are doing in horticulture and what is now available in Holland. Most people who are involved in the business are present, promoting their products and displaying to the general public and professionals alike what progress they have made in growing flowers, bulbs, vegetables and trees. In addition you are able to see the newest type of greenhouse or other equipment and some companies especially wait to launch a new product at the Floriade. The Dutch government is also there, to show their view on landscaping and ideas on planning new building areas. Experimental stations and scientists show their work, some very futuristic, as do nursery people with the newest ideas about building and managing greenhouses. You can see how flowers and vegetables are produced and of course the bulb business is very prominent.

As already indicated the Floriade is held every ten years and in 1992 was close to The Hague, but now it is situated close to Amsterdam with its airport at Schiphol. The 65 hectares (160 acres) park is large, and a major part of this will, after show closure, become a recreation area for all the people who live in the surrounding area. A smaller part specially made for the Floriade with all kinds of pavilions will be broken up and used as plots for building houses of new forms and types in park surroundings.

The Floriade is an international exhibition, so you can find many promotional displays by countries from all over the world. There is also excellent cooperation with environmental organisations, who have a very important input in the show and also have their own pavilions.

The indoor bulb show

The exhibition is in two parts; a large outside display in spring with the flower bulbs, followed by summer flowering plants, and a very big hall with 39 different indoor shows held over the season. The first of these indoor shows was for flowering bulbs and complemented the very spectacular opening on 5 April by Queen Beatrix.

Winning tulips were the fringed and double ones, Gold for 'Mazda', a dark red and fringed tulip and Gold also for 'Orange Princess', a double mutation of 'Princess Irene'. There are now available many new coloured fringed and double tulips, particularly the latter, with 'Red Princess', 'Verona' - light yellow, 'Chato' - dark pink, 'Horizon' - red with white edge, 'Globe' - pink and 'Black Hero' a double sport of 'Queen of Night'. Other remarkable tulips are a group of cultivars bred originally in the Czech Republic; 'Havran' - nearly black and 'Gavota' and 'Raijka' which are also dark coloured. Winning long-stemmed tulips were 'Flaming Parrot', 'Dordogne' a single-late sport of 'Menton', 'La Courtine' and 'World Expression'. In Hyacinths the soft colours are popular, like 'Gipsy Queen' - orange, 'Yellow Queen' and 'Top Hit' - a light blue. Winners here were 'Jan Bos' and 'Blue Jacket'. The daffodil winners were Gold for 'Border Beauty', Silver for 'Trena' and Double Gold Medal, 'Las Vegas'. Again there were more and more colours and forms that gave great interest to the public; all were arranged as cut-flowers or in pots.

The bulb season outside ended on the 25 May, all flowers were removed and most of the displays cleaned up. These displays were situated in wood-surroundings and not every exhibitor had understood what that meant, but in general the public was very enthusiastic. For our own display we designed a garden around a very nice bronze sculpture, specially made for us by an artist, Iris Le Rutte from Amsterdam (see Fig. 28). In the Autumn of 2001 we planted about 12,000 bulbs of 90 different varieties giving a good example of the range of cultivars that we grow and received a lot of positive comments.

Judging was split into two parts; part one, the displays of the individual exhibitors; part two, a special plot where every grower could plant 30 bulbs of a variety he/she liked. Unfortunately some of these plots suffered from problems with water during the winter. Winning tulips were; 'Candy Club', a multi-headed pale-yellow, 'Chato', a dark pink double, 'Red Princess', 'Princesse Charmante', a fosteriana hybrid, 'Barbados' and 'Flashback', a lily flowered tulip. Hyacinth winners were 'Blue Jacket' and 'Ibis' a new red-pink one. Daffodil winners were 'Golden Dawn', 'Cotinga', 'Reggae', 'The Alliance', Snow Frills', 'Accent', Bell Song', 'Chromacolor', 'Gamay' and 'Quail'. Another remarkable winner was *Fitillaria persica* 'Ivory Bells', the white form of this well-known black species.

Overall the Floriade was very successful for the bulb industry. Starting with the opening by the Queen, which always generates a lot of publicity and continuing with very enthusiastic reactions from the public. There were one or two negative aspects, such as long walking distances, some high prices and flower naming mainly only in Dutch. At the start there were more visitors from abroad than from our own country, but the season started early and was followed by cool weather which gave a very long flowering time. The number of visitors was high from the start and it is hoped that it will reach nearly three million visitors before closure on 20 October.

This year's Floriade shows that Holland is still at the top of the world flower industry. Floriade is a very good window to the world, and we look forward now to the next one in 2012.

Carncairn Daffodils (Broughshane)
Gold Medal Daffodils
For Exhibition and Garden

"Sally Kington"

Send For Your Free Catalogue
With a Stamped Addressed Envelope (A5 size)
To: Houston's Mill
         10a Buckna Road, Broughshane,
         Ballymena, Northern Ireland,
         BT42 4NJ
Tel: (+44) 028 2586 2805
Fax: (+44) 028 2586 2700
Email: broughshane@nacn.org
Website: www.broughshanecommunity.com

Starting A Snowdrop Collection

Matt Bishop

As novice galanthophiles, we have all at some time, thumbed wonderingly through the snowdrop vendors' seductive catalogue descriptions. As mouth-watering as they sound, the choice is far from straight forward as it is not always clear which cultivars are tried and tested and a good bet for the beginner. With this in mind, the following notes are about those snowdrops I would recommend when starting a collection from scratch, and why. All, with reasonable care, are easy to grow in a wide range of conditions, and increase freely, and are cultivars that no collection should be without. An important factor which has governed the selection for this article is availability. With time the following list will no doubt change as there are many promising cultivars appearing on the scene, but it will take some time before they have been increased sufficiently in numbers to become widely available.

The merits of *G. nivalis*, as a garden plant are well known, and its easy-going nature is also present in many of its numerous cultivars. To choose just three, I would not be without what must be by far the easiest of all virescent (green-shaded) snowdrops to grow, the small, late-flowering *G. nivalis* **'Greenish'**. Its widely splayed leaves are nicely complimented by upright scapes that carry flowers in which, as the name suggests, all segments are shaded green (see Fig. 19). Altogether more conformist in its markings for a *G. nivalis*, **'Viridapice'** has the typical V-shaped inner segment marking whilst the outer segments have bold, solid green tips; the flowers are held under an enlarged spathe which adds to the attraction of this robust, tall-growing snowdrop (see Fig. 17). Another cultivar of *G. nivalis* which is a must for any fledgling collection is **'Anglesey Abbey'**. Taking the name of the famous snowdrop garden of the National Trust near Cambridge where it is thought to have occurred, it is a plant that combines to great effect, two unusual characters: green leaves and poculiform flowers in which all six segments are pure white and of equal length; *en masse* it makes an excellent show.

G. plicatus has provided us which some very fine cultivars characterised by their broad, length wise pleated foliage and generously sized flowers; in its best forms this species has the edge in flower power over *G. nivalis* as single bulbs are capable of producing two scapes. This is certainly true of **'Washfield Warham'** which shows its large, shapely, single-marked flowers towards the end of the season. Equally eye-catching though flowering a couple weeks earlier is the refreshingly hearty **'Wendy's Gold'**, always much in demand for the bright yellow colouration of its ovary and marking on the inner segments. It is a world away from the frequently feeble similarly coloured *G. nivalis* forms now united in the Sandersii Group.

G. elwesii is as variable in size and marking as any other species; the constant factor though, is the glaucous, supervolute foliage with flat margins. Although dried and consequently short-lived imported bulbs of this species have somewhat tarnished its reputation as a garden plant, the forms with just a single mark near the apex of the inner segments have an extensive history of longevity. These plants were previously grown as *G. caucasicus*, a name fraught with taxonomic difficulties, but are now classified under var. *monostictus*; there are

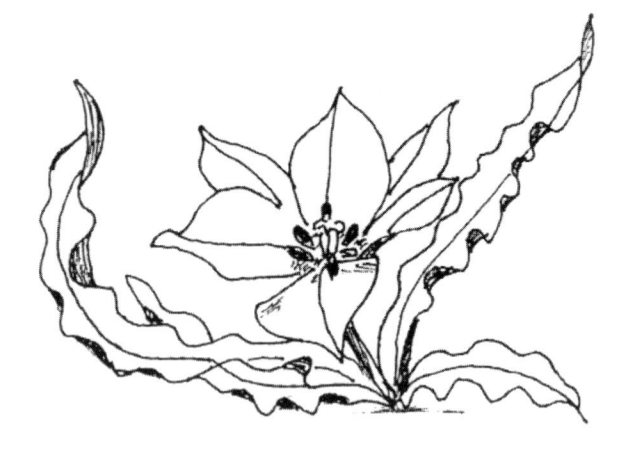

JĀNIS RUKŠĀNS
BULB NURSERY

TOP QUALITY DAFFODILS FOR EXHIBITION AND GARDEN FOR THE CHEAPEST PRICES

THE LARGEST SELECTION OF THE RAREST SMALL BULBS

TWO RICHLY ILLUSTRATED COLOUR CATALOGUES FOR ONLY US $5 BILL, REFUNDABLE WITH FIRST ORDER

J. RUKŠĀNS, P.O. ROZULA, LV-4150 CĒSIS DISTR., LATVIA
TEL/FAX: +371-41-00-326. TEL: +371-941-84-40

many cultivars but two are indispensable. Usually flowering in the first weeks of the New Year, **'Mrs McNamara'** is the clone I would have in preference to all others, epitomising the qualities that make a good snowdrop. Sturdy scapes rise well above slender leaves, and carry large, perfectly proportioned flowers of excellent substance on their strong, upright pedicels. As a close second I would choose John Morley's **'Comet'** whose generously sized flowers are carried on long arched pedicels, giving a poise not found in other var. *monostictus*. Sometimes there can be green markings towards the apex of the outer segments, but their appearance is unpredictable and in fact, they add little to an already supreme garden plant.

To collect all of the single-flowered hybrids derived from *G. nivalis* and *G. plicatus* that have a simple V-shaped marking on their inner segments would be the perfect way to create a very dull collection, but five such plants stand out for their quality. **'Bertram Anderson'** is an exemplary large flowered clone acknowledged as a fine snowdrop by its Award of Merit. With a broad inner segment marking, its substantial flowers are conspicuous for their heavy texture, regardless of the size of collection in which they appear. Few would claim to be able to identify a cultivar by its scent only but this can be said for **'Ginns' Imperati'** whose presence can be detected on a warm February day by the telltale waft of bitter almonds, even when the plants are out of sight. The movement of air also allow the easy identification of the graceful **'Magnet'** whose flowers swing about more than most snowdrops, on long, slender, arched pedicels. This snowdrop comes with a 108 year proven track record and is one of the oldest extant cultivars. Rather less senior though no less regarded, **'S. Arnott'** achieved prominence in 1951 when it received the accolade of Award of Merit from the Royal Horticultural Society. Although there is now some confusion between it and similar cultivars, stocks of 'S. Arnott' obtained from any of the specialist suppliers seem uniform and of a tall, stately snowdrop still justifying the award. From the same period,

'Ketton' was selected by one of the great galanthophiles of the twentieth century, E A Bowles and would sit well with the above single-marked hybrids were it not for the presence of two faint stains near the base of the inner segments. A tall snowdrop, its flowers are in perfect proportion but most noticeable for the smooth texture and crystalline quality of their outer segments, paired with a cast-iron constitution.

Adding another dimension, are those hybrids whose inner segment marking extends towards the base, thereby producing a marked contrast with the whiteness of the outer segments. This phenomenon has given us many good plants, but in the best of them the marking is just part of the equation. **'John Gray'** is a plant of many qualities; as well as having a beautiful "washed" marking of varied tone, its flowers are produced early in the season, are large and of good substance, carried on long arching pedicels, and often there are two scapes. This is also true of the solidly marked **'Tubby Merlin'** whose stiffly vertical scapes contrast strikingly with the almost prostrate, glaucous foliage. The tightly clasped inner segments form a tube arrangement and the ovary is bright olive green, both features that clearly betray its *G. gracilis* ancestry (see Fig. 16).

Demonstrably the toughest of all cultivars is the double-flowered form of *G. nivalis*, 'Flore Pleno' which can spread to form carpets by the hectare, and in this state, the sophistication lacking in the often-unsymmetrical individual flowers scarcely matters. Much refinement has taken place through the paternal pairing of this plant with *G. plicatus* and *G. elwesii* and happily many of these hybrids are almost as undemanding. Worth mentioning for their regular availability is the series of mostly superb garden snowdrops raised by Heyrick Greatorex of Norwich in the 1940s in which *G. plicatus* was employed as mother. Of these, my first choice would include 'Cordelia', 'Jaquenetta' and 'Titania', (the others can come later) but if only allowed one of the set, it would have to be the relatively short '**Hippolyta**' which is one of the most rounded, regular doubles, even in comparison with more recent introductions. Of similar parentage and size, though much older is '**Hill Poë**' which is immediately recognized by the five equally-spaced outer segments. The up-turned flower is distinctive also, as the inner segments are slightly flared at the apex and packed tightly together, thereby producing a neat flat, white rosette (see Fig. 18). Although grown for many years simply as *G. caucasicus* 'double', '**Lady Beatrix Stanley**' is the earliest known double-flowered hybrid of *G. nivalis* 'Flore Pleno' and *G. elwesii*, and unlike the majority that result from this combination, has only a single, reduced mark towards the apex of the inner segments, clearly visible between the fang-like "outers". As in all good doubles, the arrangement of the inner segments is fairly regular.

Having compiled the prospective shopping list may I recommend honing it a little and purchasing more of fewer different cultivars, rather than fewer of more, at least of the cheaper ones. It is, after all, far more satisfying to see good clumps of a few clones fairly quickly instead of waiting for a smattering of singletons to bulk up! Finally, do remember, that a little effort in ensuring good cultivation is repaid later; this cannot be over emphasized.

Further reading; Bishop M, Davis A P & Grimshaw J M (2001). *Snowdrops, a monograph of cultivated Galanthus*. Maidenhead: The Griffin Press. Reviewed on page 67.

RHS Show Dates 2003

Ornamental Plant Competition	January 21 22
Early Daffodil Competition	March 4 5
Daffodil Show at Wisley	April 15 16
Late Daffodil Competition	April 29 30
Tulip Competition	April 29 30

All events, with the exception of the Daffodil Show at Wisley, will be held in the New Hall, Greycoat Street, Westminster, London SW1 2PE.

The Daffodil Show at Wisley will be held at RHS Garden Wisley, Woking, Surrey GU23 6QB.

For further information contact the Shows Department, The Royal Horticultural Society, Vincent Square, London SW1P 2PE. (Telephone 020-7630-7422)

Yet Another G. elwesii? Notes on a Snowdrop from Turkey

Jörg Lebsa

Turkey is notable not only for its breathtaking countryside and witnesses of antiquity, but also for an extraordinary wealth of plants. Hot and dry summers contrasted by wet, often also very cold winters are among the causes of a special wealth of bulbous and cormous plants. This situation is emphasized by the meeting of European and Asian floras in a country of very different climatic regions and numerous, frequently isolated mountains. Away from areas of human activity an incredible mosaic of plants occurs anywhere from the shores up into the mountains of the country. Finding plants which won't fit any of the descriptions given in the *Flora of Turkey* only illustrates the vastness of the country, and the inaccessibility of many of its mountains, where many species new to science can still be found. This is also true for the snowdrops of Turkey, particularly for the multitude of the variable *G. elwesii*.

A puzzling snowdrop population

It was Joachim Sixtus of Dresden who told me about a puzzling snowdrop population he had seen south of Antalya, where the plants grew at an altitude of about 300m (1,000ft). Growing underneath an old oriental plane tree by a waterfall, the size of their leaves had struck him when he found them at the end of February, when they were about 50cm (20in) long, coming near the end of their growth, several of the plants bearing ripe seed pods. This is at odds with *G. elwesii*, which often flowers between February and April. Besides, there were no records of *G. elwesii* in the area, it being a plant of the mountains at heights of 800-1,500m (2,670-5,000ft). *G. elwesii* growing at 300m (1,000ft) in coastal regions was certainly rather unusual.

A trip to Turkey

Travelling to Turkey in October 2000 intending to study *G. peshmenii*, I decided that I should also visit the location of this strange snowdrop. The place turned out to be unusually wet and yet warm with a south easterly orientation. Temperatures at the end of October were still around a summery 25°C (77°F). If snowdrops were to flourish here, this could only be some time between November and March, with temperatures below 15°C (59°F)! *G. peshmenii* also needs the cooler season and is in growth during October/November, and dormant again by April. The problem was to time another visit if I wanted to study the mysterious plant, and obviously January could be ruled out if the plant had been bearing seed by February! A planned holiday by November 2001 was out of question so it was not until early December that I could leave Dresden for Turkey. My hopes of being in time for this snowdrop, or any snowdrop indeed, were faint; *G. peshmenii* would definitely have finished flowering by then, and the snowdrops underneath the plane tree by the waterfall could hardly be different. Stepping out into a summery 20°C (68°F) at Antalya I was so much surer that this would not be the occasion.

Not that a visit a week earlier would have been a better choice, as I was to discover. The region had been struck by a disastrous storm, and floods had not only made roads impassable with torrents of mud and rock falls, but it had also torn away roads, so that travelling was not exactly swift, with clearance still in progress. And what a spectacular waterfall it was now by the plane tree!

Found

No snowdrops, though, *Arum disocorides* instead. Still an untimely visit? At second sight there they were, however, directly by the water, mostly single plants, some still in bud, and when I started looking around, I soon found more! (see Figs 13, 14, 15)

But this certainly was no *G. elwesii*! Most plants had leaves either a mere 2-10cm (0.8-4in) long, or even still completely absent, reminding me of the various forms of *G. reginae-olgae*. The flowers were on scapes up to 20-35cm (8-14in) tall, and the flowers were large, with outer tepals at 20-44 × 10-16mm (0.8-1.8 × 0.4-0.6in). The inner tepals at 12-15 × 6-10mm (0.6-0.6 × 0.2-0.4in) were also remarkable. Who could describe my surprise when I found what could, for a *G. elwesii* at least, only be considered very unusual green marks on the inner tepals? The green mark was a single mark at the sinus, common among the *elwesii* only among those we now class as G. *caucasicus* hort., the former *caucasicus* 'Hiemalis-Group', or *G. elwesii* var. *monostictus,* but this variety had never been found in the wild and had been described from cultivated plants, and, besides, all of these were always smaller plants altogether! Their marks were a narrow ∩ or Λ; here I stood among plants reminding me of *monostictus* types such as 'Comet' or 'Miller's Late', but early December certainly would have been rather untimely for these February/March flowering plants! A rather intense and musty bitter almond scent, much more pronounced than in *G. allenii,* made these flowers even more remarkable, and certainly had nothing in common with *G. elwesii* which is described as honey scented.

I spent two more days trying to survey the area and the population size of this snowdrop. This may sound simple, but certainly was not after the good soaking the storms had given the place. A few planks across the little river were flooded or torn away, and dense scrub often forced a return. The water, though, had frequently washed free or even un-rooted the snowdrops along its banks. But there were more of them in the scrub along the fields, always at 150-300m (500-1,000ft), always in very wet places, and always warm and sheltered. How different this is from *G. peshmenii,* also growing in this part of the country, where between Antalya and Kemer it can even be found in cool gorges and in deepest shade, enduring days and even weeks under snow; and how different this was from anything we know about *G. elwesii*. Places like this one here, mild and moist in winter, and distinctly Mediterranean, are rare even in this part of Turkey. Plants growing here are *Arum dioscorides, Arisarum vulgare, Mentha* sp., *Ornithogalum* sp., *Bellevalia trifoliata, Hedera* and various *Rubus*. Soil is a fat loam overlying limestone. The snowdrops growing on richer soil were in small clumps, individual plants frequently showing two to four tiny offshoots.

A second population

I found another population further up at 650m (2,070ft), where the plants had even settled in cracks in the rock, or grew on top of large boulders. Here, *Biarum tenuifolium* joined the association I had observed further down.

My efforts to find more plants were in vain. Wherever the place looked right, warm and sheltered, and wet, I could find the other plants, but small rivers were often diverted into irrigation channels, and oleanders were taking over, and the snowdrop would appear never to make company with this evergreen, or any other evergreen plants growing here. This second population grew in a comparable south easterly position, and accordingly, there was little difference in their growth. By contrast, at the lower end of the distribution the first flowers were over, and the leaves had begun to stretch. How different this is with *G. peshmenii,* where this occurs higher up first! Those leaves had little in common with the standard *elwesii,* being much less glaucous, with the edges slightly turned under and wavy, reminding of *G. plicatus.* They are widest in their upper third, and distinctly keeled underneath. Sharing one thing with *G. elwesii* it has the typical hood-like leaf tip. Ultimately this leaf measures a remarkable 35-55cm (14-22in) in length, and 13-23mm (0.5-1in) wide. Never though, did I find a flower with the typical *elwesii* marks! The green mark would cover about a third of the tepal, rarely half; some very few plants had green spots or lines on the outer tepals. And always these flowers were large and of such exquisite proportion as to make them peer to many a cultivar of distinction!

More work needed

Quite obviously, these plants represent a relict population of a very unusual snowdrop which survived in the remoteness of its home, with encroaching farming and building activities making this a very perilous existence. It may be only a matter of years rather than of decades before this splendid plant is reduced to some few individuals.

Whatever this snowdrop may be in relation to others, it is quite different from those we are familiar with. It is also different from what we call *G. elwesii* var. *monostictus,* a plant described from cultivated plants of what is thought to be a southern Turkish (Taurus) origin. Further investigations will be necessary to gain more understanding of this plant, and it may become necessary to recognize it as something new, differing from *G. elwesii* and var. *monostictus* in its mode of growth, its flowering time, size, and scent.

© Jörg Lebsa 2002. Translation from the German original: Karl-Heinz Neuwirth This text was first published in a slightly extended version (in German) as: Jörg Lebsa, "Nur ein weiteres *Galanthus elwesii?* - Anmerkungen zu einem türkischen Schneeglöckchen", in: *Gartenbotanische Blätter* 5.2002, Gartenbotanische Vereinigung Hildesheim, July 2002.

RINGHADDY DAFFODILS

Incorporating

Ballydorn Bulb Farm
and
Brian Duncan Daffodils

New catalogue available from February 2003

Listing Ballydorn & Brian Duncan Daffodil varieties and new releases, with many more from other top hybridisers.

Please send for colour catalogue enclosing £2.50, which is redeemable against order.

Nial and Hilary Watson,
Ringhaddy Daffodils
Killinchy
Co. Down
BT23 6TU.
Northern Ireland.

Tel: 028 9754 1007.   Fax: 028 9752 276
email: ringdaff@nireland.com

Daffodil, Snowdrop and Tulip Yearbook 2002-2003

Fig. 1 (above): 'Cantabile' (see p.20).
Fig. 2 (right): 'Vienna Woods' (see p.25).

Fig. 3 (left): 'Chesterton' (see p.28).
Fig. 4 (above): The controversial 'Killearnan' (see p.21).

Daffodil, Snowdrop and Tulip Yearbook 2002-2003

Fig. 5 (left): 'Eastbrook Sunrise' Best Bloom and Best Unregistered Seedling (G-001) at the RHS Early Daffodil Competition (see p.81). Fig. 6 (above): 'Trimon' as seen by Alan Edwards at the AGS Early Spring Show Harlow (see p.94). Fig. 7 (below left): 'Dandubar' Reserve Best Bloom and Best Miniature at the RHS Early Daffodil Competition (see p.81). Fig. 8 (below): 'Jodi' Best Unregistered Seedling (1736) and Best Division 11 at the RHS Daffodil Show (see p.87)

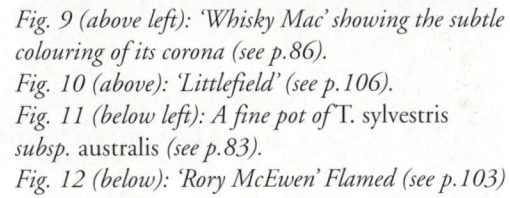

Daffodil, Snowdrop and Tulip Yearbook 2002-2003

Fig. 9 (above left): 'Whisky Mac' showing the subtle colouring of its corona (see p.86).
Fig. 10 (above): 'Littlefield' (see p.106).
Fig. 11 (below left): A fine pot of T. sylvestris subsp. australis (see p.83).
Fig. 12 (below): 'Rory McEwen' Flamed (see p.103)

Daffodil, Snowdrop and Tulip Yearbook 2002-2003

Three examples of 'G. elwesii?' Fig. 13 (above left): green-tipped form. Fig. 14 (above right): showing green markings on inner tepals. Fig. 15 (below): growing near a rock.

Fig. 16 (above): 'Tubby Merlin' (see p.59)

Fig. 17 (above): 'Viridapice' (see p.57)

Fig. 18 (above): 'Hill Pöe' (see p.60)

Fig. 19 (above): 'Greenish' (see p.57)

Fig. 20 (left): N. dubius *growing on a little rocky hill near Santa Eulalia (see p.14). Fig. 21 (above):* N. triandrus *subsp.* pallidulus *with a split corona, which John Blanchard found 'curiously attractive' (see p.16). Fig. 22 (below): A fine clump of* N. cyclamineus *growing near Sigueiro (see p.14).*

Daffodil, Snowdrop and Tulip Yearbook 2002-2003

Fig. 23 (left): N. × montserratii *growing on a steep north-facing hillside just below Arties in the Val d'Aran (see p.17).* Fig. 24 (above): N. × cazorlanus *'At it's best this is a pretty little flower sometimes with two in a stem…' (see p.15).* Fig. 25 (below): N. cyclamineus *growing beneath trees on the banks of the Rio Timbre (see p.14).*

Fig. 26 (left): Elise Havens to whom the RHS awarded the Peter Barr Memorial Cup in 2002 (see p.65). Fig. 27 (above): Part of a display of tulips by Bloms Bulbs at the RHS Chelsea Show.

Fig. 28 (above): Jan Pennings de Bilt display at the Floriade.

The Peter Barr Memorial Cup 2002 Awarded to Mrs Elise Havens

Elise Havens is the daughter of the late Grant E Mitsch whose name has been synonymous with daffodils since he started hybridizing in 1934 and supplying them to enthusiasts in 1945. Elise and her husband Richard have been running Grant Mitsch Novelty Daffodils since 1973, steadily building and enhancing the firm's reputation as the primary suppliers of top quality and novel daffodils in America. Elise (see Fig. 26) now proudly follows her illustrious father as the most recent winner of this most prestigious award - Grant Mitsch was awarded the Cup in 1973. She would also want to acknowledge the major contribution that Richard has made to their accomplishments.

With her father's encouragement Elise started making her own crosses at an early age, and some 15 cultivars were registered and catalogued between 1975 and 1979, perhaps the best known being 'Graduation' 2W-WWP and 'Pay Day' 1 YYW-W. There was then a break until the early 1990s, presumably because Elise had left to pursue another career. Since that time more than 100 cultivars have been registered, covering most divisions. Famous amongst these have been the break-through crosses in yellow/pink trumpets and large cups: 'American Heritage' 1YYW-P, 'American Dream' 1Y-P and 'Oregon Pioneer' 2Y-P; and the fertile Jonquilla hybrids which open a door to further progress and development of colours in the higher divisions. Meanwhile split-corona daffodils have been brought to a new level of refinement and acceptance. Numerous excellent daffodils of other types are also gracing show benches and the gardens of enthusiasts throughout the world.

Elise Havens does not regard competitive exhibition of daffodils as a high priority activity. However, her customers do this job so effectively for her that Havens cultivars are dominant in USA shows and are widely exhibited elsewhere.

Elise is a director of the American Daffodil Society, and is currently Chairman of the Standing Committee on Hybridizing. She has been a regular contributing speaker at ADS conventions and Chairman of the annual Hybridizers' Breakfast. She received the ADS Gold Medal in 1997.

Elise Havens has travelled widely, including to the United Kingdom, and has exhibited at the London Daffodil Show on at least two occasions. She is a wonderful ambassador for daffodils and her country. Deep thinking, charming and generous, the ever-smiling Elise has made a host of friends in daffodil circles throughout the world. She is "Queen of Daffodils" in her homeland, and she is arguably the world's most outstanding hybridizer, producing as she does, wonderful new daffodils in practically the whole range of daffodil divisions in the Classified List.

It was my pleasure to announce that Elise Havens was the recipient of the Peter Barr Memorial Cup for 2002 and to present a framed picture of the Cup to her at the American Daffodil Society Convention in Cincinnati.

The popularity of the RHS decision was illustrated by the standing ovation accorded to Elise.

Brian Duncan

OBITUARY

JOHN DANIEL DU PLESSIS

All in the daffodil and horticultural industries together with the amateur daffodil fraternity around the world were deeply shocked and saddened by the news that Dan du Plessis had died on 20 September 2001. He was aged 77. His death followed an operation to replace a hip that had for some time caused him pain and prevented him from enjoying his garden and daffodils to the full. A picture of Dan was published in *Daffodils and Tulips* 1994-5 (see Fig. 15). Dan was a keen horticulturalist and naturalist, interested in all aspects of the countryside and the community, and all his life had worked to help and improve the environment and surroundings we live in.

Dan was born at Marsh Farm in the Tamar Valley and he lived there all his working life. It was then a mixed farm with some livestock, but primarily fruit and cut flowers; growing daffodils, anemones, violets and much more. In 1943 he took over the management and running of the farm in partnership with his brother Peter, until their retirement in 1991. They built up a substantial acreage of daffodils both for the cut flower trade and as speciality bulbs for discerning gardeners and exhibitors.

Dan was a highly respected member of his community, his civic duties including service on the Landulph Parish Council for 27 years, 9 of them as Chairman. He was devoted to his family and to his church where he was instrumental in promoting the church restoration appeal. His knowledge and love of the daffodil was to lead him to several prominent positions in the daffodil industry. He served for many years together with his wife Eileen, as secretary to the Tamar Valley Show until its demise in 1967, and as representative on the National Farmers Union's Bulb Committee for the South West of England. Dan also served for many years on the selection committee at the Rosewarne Experimental Horticulture Station. A member of the Royal Horticultural Society's Daffodil and Tulip Committee for 19 years and its Classification Advisory Committee for 11 years, Dan was awarded in 1984 the Peter Barr Cup in recognition of his work with daffodils. He was a Vice President of the Daffodil Society, and served on its Committee for many years where his knowledge of both historical and modern daffodils was invaluable. He was a director and founder member of CABGA a specialist group of daffodil growers in Cornwall.

Over the years Dan, forever the showman, had sought and acquired a great many new and exciting daffodils with the future in mind. He had a fine eye for the best and strongest plants with potential for the garden and especially for the flower trade. Many became very successful varieties on the show benches and are now also prominent in the bulb industry. To mention only a few, 'Tamar Fire', 'Gay Kybo' and 'Bere Ferrers', raised by Mrs H K Richardson but registered by Dan and his brother in 1980, 1976 and 1979 repectively, are not only sold as cut flowers but also as bulbs to exhibitors. In recent years Dan had more time to spend hybridizing and raised many new and different cultivars, which I am pleased to be growing on and will be able to introduce in the future.

Dan, was of course not only my uncle and my mentor but also a close pal, and was affectionately known by many within the daffodil show fraternity as "Uncle Dan". He is sadly missed by all who knew him, and everyone he met he left as a friend.

Ron Scamp

Book Reviews

Snowdrops: A Monograph of Cultivated Galanthus. by Matt Bishop, Aaron Davis and John Grimshaw. The Griffin Press, Maidenhead, 2001. £45 (pp xi + 364 including 218 colour plates).

F C Stern's *Snowdrops and Snowflakes* was published by the Royal Horticultural Society in 1956. Two new generations of gardeners with their selections and collections has made it long in need of revision, so a new book has been eagerly awaited by the small but intensely enthusiastic band of snowdrop cultivators. However this monograph does more than lay a few ghosts; it is very accessible to the beginner, with its clear and concise coverage doing away with much of the mystic of "the semi-double with striped green outers found in the stable yard of some famous late gardener" who naturally can hardly refute the fable.

Writing the section on the species has enabled Aaron Davis to update *The Genus Galanthus* published as recently as 1999. The bulk of the text is devoted to over five hundred cultivars and the numerous synonyms. These are the subjective choice of the authors, especially Matt Bishop who systematically checked them all. One of the joys of this book is in the small print description of each cultivar. This description is very clear and succinct, with an extremely useful ratio given of the ovary, comparing the width with the length, maybe not in every botanical treatise, but just right for the gardener. The book has many almost standardised cameo photographs of the flower heads of selected snowdrops. It would have been even better to have a photograph next to each description, but that maybe is too much to ask.

Research has been painstakingly undertaken, giving the history of each cultivar, including its commercial availability. The cultivars are indexed under their species affiliation and then under a section for cultivars unattributable to any species. This is sometimes a little frustrating and tends to lead to a trawl through each section, especially if you are unfamiliar with the plant. Otherwise the index is very clear with good use of bold and ordinary type, leaving no doubt in the mind of the reader as to the correct name. The chapter on "Galanthophiles and Galanthophilia" has some interesting insights into the growers of past generations, highlighting the fact that the high prices associated with new and rare snowdrops are nothing new. The cultivation of the genus is covered in full, as are the various forms of propagation, including twin-scaling, which does at least begin to address the great demand for the choicest snowdrops.

Overall this book looks and feels just right; it has not had to fit into a series and meet the resulting constraints, and has been designed and produced to fit the subject and that it does very well.

Rod Leeds

Tulip by Liz Dobbs. Photography by Clay Perry, Consultant Cees Breed. Quadrille, London, 2002. £12.99 (pp 104)
Tulips by Sonia Day. Photography Malak Karsh. Key Porter Books, Canada, 2002. $24.95 (pp 128)

At first glance Liz Dobbs' *Tulip* stirs you with the anticipation of a wonderful tulip experience. Unfortunately this for me was unfulfilled. It's a curious book. The work of two, or possibly three people, it seems as if each has done their own little bit independently of the others. The book is in three parts. The first five pages relate to the history with the obligatory tulipomania and English Florist tulips in beer bottles.

Her unease is apparent in her inability to spell bybloemen. There are no photographs of broken tulips and an opportunity to demonstrate the difference between a virus infected flower and a flower bred with streaks is missed. The couple of pages covering the classification checklist serve as an index for the second and main part of the book.

The next seventy-three pages are devoted to superb photographs of tulips from the collection of Cees Breed. There is generally one cultivar per page and each is a silhouette on the white page, accompanied by a brief description of breeding, height, flowering time etc. Unfortunately working through seventy-three such pages is like perusing a lengthy up-market bulb catalogue with no indication of availability.

The most worrying aspect is the lack of shape in the work. Cultivars are presented at random with no attempt at organisation based on classification, flowering time, colour etc. If Darwinhybrids, as it states, are the second most widely grown type in Holland, why are only two cultivars described among the seventy-three on offer?

There are a few positive things to be winkled out of the various descriptions. Both 'Maureen' and 'Renown' are seedlings from 'Mrs John T Scheepers', while in turn 'Menton' is a sport of 'Renown'. The importance of sports in the tulips we grow is undersold, and more could have been made of it. There are snippets there, but they are bitty and disjointed.

The final thirteen pages are devoted to tulips in the garden. To be told that tulips can be underplanted with wallflowers or forget-me-nots hardly breaks new ground.

I suppose this is what is called a "coffee table book"! Pick it up, flick a few pages, marvel at the beautiful pictures, but don't expect to learn much.

Sonia Day's presentation *Tulips* again relies heavily on some excellent photography, this time from the late Malak Karsh. They present a more varied scene ranging from the Hortus Bulborum, the Keukenhof, the Dutch bulb fields and the formal plantings in Ottawa, which commemorate the special relationship between Canada and the Dutch Royal Family who spent the war there.

Technically the book can be faulted in that the author doesn't seem to know the difference between Darwin tulips (now included in the Single Late Group) and Darwinhybrids; also the captions do not always match the pictures. This is a book aimed at the North American market. Combating squirrels demands a great deal of attention. Overall, of the two volumes, this is the more informative and easy read, free of all pretensions.

Richard Smales

The Daffodil Society *Cultural Guide and Show Handbook (Fourth Edition)* *

The fact that this is a fourth edition speaks volumes. Like a fine malt whisky we are able to observe the results of careful distillation and a lengthy maturation process. The end product is full of sage advice, good sense, and down-to-earth conclusions. Those responsible are to be congratulated on an excellent publication.

The copy supplied to me was in loose-leaf A5 form - a good way of allowing the various sections to be regularly reviewed and updated. There are five sections consisting of: -

(A) **Daffodil classification** which was accompanied by excellent colour photographs of flowers from each division with accompanying explanatory notes. (B) **Show schedule** consisting of helpful notes for the compilers of the key document for shows. (C) **Judging of exhibition daffodils and practical procedures** which deal with getting an appropriate result from the most controversial area of daffodil growing. (D) **Open ground cultivation and pot growing of exhibition daffodils, and getting the best results from show flowers** and finally (E) **Control of pests and diseases.**

While the last of these sections is a brief summary of the vast field of literature available it does cover the major problems growers face.

Some references to more detailed accounts such as Ted Snazelle's work for those who are unlucky enough to encounter one or more of the problems would be very helpful. I am especially interested in so-called neck rot - a section on sclerotinia would be valuable here. I would also suggest that more details on hot water treatment should be added. The required temperature for dealing with pests such as narcissus fly and nematodes would be very useful for amateur growers.

I was much taken with the section on pot growing. This is an art form in the United Kingdom and is practised successfully by only a few growers in New Zealand. On my first visit to England I was very impressed with the skill of Tony Noton in this field. I could not believe the amount of endeavour and skill he used in shifting the pots around various locations to get the best results. I remember a marvellous pot of 'Sabine Hay', which Down-Under burns before it opens. I reckon he had it in his cellar until the last possible moment. The ability of United Kingdom growers generally in timing flowers for shows is not matched anywhere else in the world. I am sure that more than a handful of growers here will read this section several times!

However, the section of most interest to me was Part C, which was the subject of an international symposium in this year's *New Zealand Daffodil Annual*. Let me say from the outset that Part C is well written and forcefully argued and I agree with almost everything that appears in it. While I have very few quibbles there are, though, some areas deserving further discussion. First of these is "size for cultivar". It is interesting to note that the Daffodil Society's points scale gives double the weighting for this criterion than either the New Zealand or American systems. While I prefer well-grown flowers I believe that form is paramount and that some of the points allocated for size could be redistributed to form. I also worry about size *for cultivar*. This poses major problems for judges who do not grow a wide range of varieties, and moreover is impossible to ascertain for new seedlings. In my book a slightly under-size but otherwise excellent 'Achduart' should always beat 'Triple Crown' which almost qualifies for intermediate status! This area will always be problematic - personally I would delete the "for cultivar" and encourage breeders to focus a bit more on size.

Another controversial area is "show as registered". While this solves some problems it creates others. The Australian and Royal Horticultural Society's systems of "judge as shown" also has it difficulties. I cannot agree with a system as in Australia where many marginal flowers are measured, and re-measured at shows! On the other hand I have some sympathy with the "judge as shown" when it comes to colouration. There are many examples of colour variations according to seasonal or cultivation differences. There are even some cultivars such as 'Bandit', which will have a range of hues from bright gold to clear orange when grown in the same row and of the same maturity. I also wonder what judges do when faced with a 7Y-Y flower of 'Stratosphere' (the example given in the Manual) when shown, as the Society requires in the class for 7Y-O. It should score very few points for colour! On balance I believe "judge as shown" has considerable merit when it comes to colour considerations.

Finally, I am in full agreement with the addition of 10 per cent of points for multi-vase classes, such points to be allocated for coverage of divisions/colour combinations, and presentation. We have no such system in New Zealand other than these considerations coming into play when competition is close.

The section on practical procedures - more specifically "judging procedures" - is another very good section. It is interesting to note that the suggestions here parallel closely the procedures recommended by American, New Zealand, and Australian contributors to the *New Zealand Daffodil Annual*. A good case for international accord!

In conclusion may I congratulate the Publications Committee of the Daffodil Society on a job well done. I hope that in New

Zealand we can use their efforts as a model for a similar manual designed for our conditions - and beliefs!

Peter Ramsay, New Zealand

* Available in loose-leaf form (currrently pp44 incl 17 colour plates) to fit any two-ring A5 binder from The Daffodil Society, 70 Wrenthorpe Lane, Wrenthorpe, Wakefield, West Yorks WF2 0PT. Price £3.50 including postage and packing.

New Zealand Daffodil Annual 2002. Published by the National Daffodil Society of New Zealand. (76pp.)

As the *Yearbook* was going to press the editor received the *New Zealand Daffodil Annual 2002* which contains a 49 page international symposium on judging daffodils. National perspectives on judging are given by David Jackson (Australia); David Adams, Wilf Hall and Max Hamilton (New Zealand); James Akers and Malcolm Bradbury (United Kingdom); and Naomi Liggett and Bob Spotts (United States of America). The symposium is drawn together by the editor Peter Ramsay with a summary, conclusions and recommendations. We will publish a full review next year. In the meantime daffodil judges and exhibitors will find the symposium an informative and thought provoking read. The *Annual* is distributed free to members of the National Daffodil Society of New Zealand. Membership enquires should be sent to Mr. W T Hall, Honorary Secretary, The National Daffodil Society of New Zealand (Inc), 105 Wallace Loop Road, Ihakara, R.D.I, Levin 5500, New Zealand.

Editor

American Daffodil Society *Illustrated Databank (Version 3)* *

This is not a book, but a database loaded onto your computer from a CD. Like most software that one tries to install it didn't work first time but I persevered and eventually succeeded. The effort was well worthwhile. There are 15,443 cultivars or species included, with photographs of more than 4,000 of these. The initial screen shows cultivars in alphabetical order with five data fields: Flower name - Class (eg 2W-P) - Seed Parent - Pollen Parent and Breeder. If you don't want the cultivars in this order then you can sort them by any of the fields mentioned and by others such as the flowering season. The software is extremely powerful and one can find an individual cultivar, or even all the cultivars raised by a particular hybridizer, in less than two seconds.

Choosing a cultivar provides a screen of data including the photograph if available. Not all the photographs are of the highest quality but that can only improve with the rapid development of digital cameras. The additional data on this screen, includes where available; season, variation, height, fertility and chromosome count. Also shown are the country of origin and registration data, which may be slightly at odds with that published in *The International Daffodil Register and Classified List*. There is a remarks field which, in the case of Max Hamilton's 'Abbey Elizabeth' 4Y-P, shows that "the perianth opens creamy white, becoming lemon; corona pale pink". All information including the photograph can be printed.

However the most impressive button on which to click is marked History which immediately produces along with the photograph, an hierarchical family tree of the previous four generations of parents, where known. Clicking on any of the parents, grand parents or great grand parents then gives the data, including photograph, of that cultivar.

A very useful facility is the Growers List that enables you to flag for easy access any cultivars that you grow, and provides a screen to record your own data for each cultivar.

I have been sent a review copy valid for only six months. I don't want to send it back!

James Akers

* *Available from the American Daffodil Society. Send a cheque for $150 to Naomi Liggett, 4126 Winfield Rd., Columbus, OH 43220, USA.*

Daffodil and Snowdrop Notes

American Daffodil Society Honours Sally Kington

The American Daffodil Society (ADS) has awarded its Gold Medal to Sally Kington, the International Daffodil Registrar. The Gold Medal is awarded to an individual in "recognition of creative work of a pre-eminent nature in the understanding and advancement of daffodils".

Within three years of becoming Registrar, Sally produced the *International Daffodil Checklist* in 1989. Nine years later Sally completed the extremely comprehensive *International Daffodil Register and Classified List 1998*, which is known to daffodil enthusiasts worldwide as the "big yellow book". In the course of this work Sally has also been involved in changes to and clarifications of the classification system, including pioneering work on the boundaries between yellow, orange, pink and red. In the course of this work Sally has fostered good working relationships with daffodil registrars and enthusiasts worldwide. She has also taken a leading role in ad-hoc issues such as the "Gibside Saga" (see page 37) and been Secretary of the RHS's Daffodil and Tulip Committee since 1996.

The medal was given to Sally in a surprise presentation between committee meetings at the RHS in June. Making the presentation on behalf of the ADS, Mary Lou Gripshover referred to Sally having "accomplished so much" and to her "lasting international contributions to the Daffodil World". The RHS awarded the Peter Barr Memorial Cup to Sally in 2001 for her work with the daffodil. (See *Daffodil and Tulip Yearbook 2001-2002*, page 40 and Fig. 21).

Malcolm Bradbury

Are These Miniature Daffodils Extinct?
Delia Bankhead

I am trying to determine if any of these miniatures are still grown anywhere. All but 'Atom' were registered before 1958 and I have been unable to locate **true** stocks of any of them. I would particularly like to hear from anyone overseas who may be growing them. In the USA, there were bulbs that circulated under some of the names below, but these have either never bloomed, or turned out to be another cultivar. If true stocks of any of these cannot be located by the end of this year, the names will be dropped from the *ADS Approved Miniatures List* as lost to cultivation.

'Atom' 6Y-Y
'Peaseblossom' 7Y-Y
'Picarillo' 2Y-Y
'Sea Gift' 7Y-Y
'Skiffle' 7Y-Y (not the tall, round 'Sun Disc' look-alike sometimes seen as 'Skiffle')
'Snug' 1W-W (not the mislabelled bulbs that bloomed as 'Minnow')
'Tweeny' 2Y-Y (not the Australian or New Zealand stock that was actually 'Yellow Xit')

It is important to point out that if the breeding of 'Skiffle' was correctly recorded by Alec Gray, and I think we must assume it was, then the tall, round, nearly flat-cupped, very late flower referred to above, cannot possibly be 'Skiffle'. Both parents, *N. asturiensis* and *N. calcicola,* are very early flowers that bloom on short stems. Gray's catalogue description states the height as 76mm (3in), and in another place the flower is described as having rather long cups, which makes perfect sense, given the seed parent. I believe the real 'Skiffle' is no longer grown anywhere.

In the case of 'Tweeny,' there are a few bulbs circulating under this name in the USA, but whether or not they represent true stock of this cultivar remains to be seen. Whatever the cultivar is, it is not very vigorous and is a very shy bloomer. When it does bloom, it is nearly always two-headed, so either the name or the classification must be incorrect. If it can be established that all the bulbs labelled 'Tweeny' growing anywhere in the world match the description given here, then I think the classification should be changed to either division 7 or division 12 This flower is clearly not a division 2. The 'Tweeny' I know has a muddy white perianth, an expanded and fairly long pale yellow cup and always has two florets. I am not certain if the smaller back petals are always present, but if they are, they would serve as another aid to identification. This characteristic is not very common.

Will anyone who is growing, or who knows of the existence of any of these, please contact ADS Miniatures Chairman: Delia Bankhead, 118 Chickadee Circle, Hendersonville, NC 28792. Telephone is 828-697-8122, and e-mail address is deliab@ioa.com

Please send a photograph of the flower, if at all possible.

A New Yellow Snowdrop
Ruby Baker

Visitors to Dr Ronald Mackenzie's garden in Shilton regularly admire the early flowering *galanthus* hybrid 'Daglingworth', but last year his friends were privileged to see a form of it with ovary, basal and apical marks of a rich egg-yolk yellow. It was a stunning snowdrop and by common consent was immediately named 'Ronald Mackenzie' (see Back Cover). By means of twin-scaling it is already in the pipeline; and will no doubt be eagerly awaited by enthusiasts.

The Cottage Garden Society
Snowdrop Group
Daphne Chappell

Today, gardening societies with members whose interests cover a wide range of plants now run specialist groups. For gardeners with a particular interest in *Galanthus*, The Cottage Garden Society, quick to recognise that snowdrops were enjoying a huge renaissance, launched its Snowdrop Group.

Dedicated gardeners need flowers to enjoy at all times of the year and many grow native woodland snowdrops to enjoy during the winter months. However the Snowdrop Group caters for those who interest is in lesser-known snowdrops such as those introduced from central and southern Europe over the last 200 years. The past decade has seen an enormous interest in species and cultivar snowdrops and the group aims to promote them as equally good garden plants with advice on where to see and how best to grow them. Plant sales at the group's annual meetings are now recognised as the best source of lesser-known and rare snowdrops with leading bulb specialists invited to sell. Arranged visits for members have included a trip to the National Plant Collection of *Galanthus* in Shropshire and to an Oxfordshire snowdrop garden in the process of restoration after 70 years of neglect where many new hybrids were discovered. The day is held at a different venue each year and usually includes a lecture by a well-known plantsman.

The group published its first newsletter in January 1995 with a foreword by the expert plantsman and long time galanthophile Chris Brickell. Members are kept informed through both a November newsheet containing details of the following year's snowdrop days and open gardens nation-wide and a second, January newsletter usually profiling a particular snowdrop, plus help on identification and cultivation for new collectors.

Details of the Cottage Garden Society and the Snowdrop Group are available from Daphne Chappell, Cinderdine Cottage, Dymock, Glos. GL18 2DG.

NARCISSUS DUBIUS AS BREEDING MATERIAL
PETER BRANDHAM

Narcissus dubius is a very peculiar plant. The species is a stabilised interspecific hybrid of wild origin that breeds true to type and is the only known example of a fertile allohexaploid in the genus. It has 50 chromosomes in six sets (AAAAPP), of which four sets of seven (AAAA = 28) come from *N. assoanus* and two sets of eleven (PP = 22) come from *N. papyraceus*. It is fertile because its meiosis is regular. Each *papyraceus* chromosome has one identical one to pair with (and separate) and each *assoanus* chromosome has three identical ones to pair with (and separate into twos). So the *papyraceus* component behaves as a diploid and the *assoanus* component behaves as a tetraploid. The gametes of *N. dubius* are therefore genetically AAP, with 7 + 7 + 11 = 25 chromosomes and will be balanced and viable.

N. dubius can be crossed successfully with tetraploids of divisions 1-3 and features in the parentage of such well known miniatures as 'Crevette' 8W-O ('Mahmoud' × *N. dubius*) and Shillingstone ('Ringstead' × *N. dubius*). The tetraploids have four sets of seven chromosomes and are genetically NNNN, their gametes being NN (= 14). Their hybrids with *N. dubius* will therefore be pentaploid (AANNP) with four sets of seven (AANN) and one set of eleven (P), making 39 chromosomes overall.

Will these hybrids be fertile? Not very, I'm afraid. During their meiosis much will go well, with each A chromosome pairing with another A and each N pairing with another N. No problem so far, with the gametes being basically AN (= 14 chromosomes), but the problem is the single set of eleven P chromosomes in the AANNP hybrids. These will have nothing with which to pair while the A and N chromosomes are pairing and separating normally. They will usually separate roughly into two groups at the first meiotic separation, and the hybrids' gametes will therefore be AN (7 + 7 = 14) plus odd P chromosomes averaging, 5 or 6. This chromosomal imbalance will render most of the gametes sterile.

Despite their low fertility, it nevertheless might be worth attempting to cross the AANNP hybrids further, using something fertile as the other parent. The hybrids will produce occasional gametes with AN (= 14) plus one or another of the extremes of the range of P chromosomes (0, 1, 10, or 11) instead of the non-viable average of 5 - 6. These gametes have a good chance of being viable, because their genetic imbalance is reduced, and if they result in a successful fertilisation they would give an interesting range of further progeny with differing amounts of *papyraceus* characteristics ranging from practically nil to quite a significant quantity.

Overseas Show Reports

Daffodil Shows in New Zealand

2001 was a special year in New Zealand as the National Daffodil Society celebrated its 75th birthday. As befitted the occasion a beautifully decorated birthday cake was generously supplied by the National President, Brian Parr and his wife Pat at the two national shows held this year in Wanganui and Dunedin. The two longest standing members of the Society - Spud Brogden in the North Island and John Hunter in the South cut the cakes.

Overall it was a very good season - lots of good flowers and two very well organised national shows. The hosting was "spot on" - excellent dinners and a 75th birthday well and truly celebrated.

Commemorative Classes
The Society also decided to commemorate its 75th birthday with two special classes in each Island, for twelve varieties from at least four New Zealand raisers in the Open classes, and six varieties from at least three New Zealand raisers for the amateur growers. The Society supplied handsome prizes of engraved crystal for the place-getters in each of these classes.

In the North Island there were five excellent entries in the Open class, with Koanga Daffodils the clear winners from Spud Brogden and the Millers. Koanga had six New Zealand raisers represented in their set including Brogden, Chambers, Crotty, Verry, and the two partners in the firm, Ramsay and Hamilton. It was good to see Mavis Verry's 1Y-Y 'Lordship' still holding its own with the best in this entry. Max Hamilton's seedling 24-95, an imposing large and smooth 2Y-Y went one better than the premier achieved in 2000, taking the top award of Best Bloom in show. Two other flowers from this class also made their way to the premier table - Peter Ramsay's 96:37 a good 2W-Y bred from 'Irish Mist' × 'Flash Affair' and 'Snowy Morn' from Brogden Bulbs, thus adding to its already impressive list of victories. Tazetta expert, Wilf Hall, thought Spud unlucky not to pick up a second premier with a beautiful flower of John Byrne's seedling 86/91 an 8Y-OR. Special mention must also be made of John McLennan's unplaced entry - he really got into the spirit of the occasion with twelve different Kiwi raisers represented in his entry.

Only two growers, John Hollever and Wayne Hughes, found enough blooms to enter in the amateurs. John was a narrow winner over Wayne's two entries. While Wayne had some very strong flowers, poor examples of 'Alpine Express' and 'Polar Morn' cost him dearly in the final comparison with John's very even set.

In the South Island the reverse was the case - the Open commemorative class was disappointing with no South Island growers entering. It was left to three North Islanders to support this important class, and with one exhibitor being disqualified, a fine trophy was left unclaimed. Koanga Daffodils were once again clear winners with five raisers this time represented in their entry - Brogden, Ramsay, O'More, Hamilton and Bramley. Graham and Faith Miller completing the quinella for Waikato growers with flowers raised by Brogden, Hunter, Miller, and Crotty.

There were six good entries from amateur growers. Malcolm Wheeler and Rozanne Burnby (now showing as Malroze) put together a lovely set to win comfortably. Their set included the efforts of five hybridizers with Max Hamilton's new 4W-P 'People's Princess' and Len Chambers' 'Springston Remembrance' standing out. Alistair Davey also had a nice set which included the rarely seen 'Cameo Prince', 2W-Y and 'Centrefold', while Greg Inwood completed the place-getters - we especially liked 'Capree Elizabeth' a 2Y-P which is difficult to beat in its class.

North Island
To return to the North Island. The Wanganui show was about average in size with 1,768 blooms staged. The quality though was very good with plenty of excellent flowers on display. The Rhodes Challenge Cup for 12 varieties, New Zealand raised, was won for the fourteenth year in succession by Koanga Daffodils, from Brogden Bulbs and Graeme and Faith Miller. The winning entry was very colourful with some excellent doubles included. The most popular class in the Open Collections was for nine blooms from division 6. Malroze won with good flowers of 'Perky', 'Phalarope' and 'Mangaweka', Michael Brown was second with 'Rapture' and 'Tracey', and David Adams was third with 'Perky', 'Utiku' and 'Abracadabra'.

The other collection classes were well supported. Koanga Daffodils retained most of the trophies with large, colourful flowers. Brogden Bulbs continued their domination of the raised by exhibitor class with a beautifully staged set including the showy 'Egmont Charm', and 'Capree Elizabeth'. Graham Phillips' second placed entry was well up to standard, with 'Champeen', 2W-Y, perhaps the best of his flowers. The Millers were third with an entry composed entirely of cyclamineus hybrids. John Hollever continued his successful move to the open grade with three wins including the bicolour trumpets, division 2 and 3 all-whites, and the small cups. IRN Associates (the Irwins) won the Wilson Trophy for white trumpets with a good set. Unfortunately the best entry here, from the Millers, was disqualified as two of their seedlings failed to meet trumpet measurements.

The Miniature Daffodil Championship was won by David Adams from Sue and Colin Reid and Malroze. David's own 'Saturn Five' was in good form in his entry. Also noted were good examples of 'Angel's Whisper', a fine introduction from Rod Barwick of Tasmania. There were only a few entries in the intermediates; Robin Hill showed nice examples of 'Red Atom', 2Y-O, which appeared to be a genuine intermediate contender.

The amateur collections were dominated by Wayne Hughes- his entry in the Waikato Challenge Tray was one of the best seen in recent years. The hard to grow 'Dorchester' was outstanding in this entry, as was 'Gold Bond'. Andrew Jenkins, staged a very even twelve which narrowly beat Kevin Sherlock into third place. Kevin's entry included a lovely flower of 'New Penny' which was Reserve Best Bloom in show. One of the nicest entries in the Amateurs was in the newly donated Don Stuart Memorial Trophy for Australian raised cultivars. This was won by Andrew Jenkins with six blooms all raised by Jacksons of Tasmania. Especially impressive were 'No Worries' and 'Impeccable'. The amateur threes were heavily contested by Kevin Johnston and Ralph Mountford with the former taking the Taranaki Rosebowl for most points. Ralph's flowers get better every year; fine examples of 'Cameo Baron', 2Y-R, and 'Sheelagh Rowan' caught our attention. Bill Robottom and Bill Mcleod both showed quality blooms in the amateur singles, with Miriam Miller (a recent graduate from the children's grades), Kevin Sherlock, Brian McKenzie, E and H Lane, A and R Hannam and Natalie Mc Farlane all recording wins.

The Premier stand was well up to standard. Flowers which stood out were 'Trumpet Warrior' (Wayne Hughes), the problematic 'Lady Di' (Koanga), 'Shykoski' (G and F Miller) and 'Puhoi', a fine jonquilla raised by the late Robin Brown. Andrew Jenkins took three of the amateur premiers - his 'No Worries' was the Best Amateur Bloom in show, and Amelia Hooker's 'Pukenui' was best in the children's section.

South Island
On to Dunedin where the local horticultural society was celebrating its 150th anniversary. The show was held in a large, roomy stadium

with very good lighting; 2,343 blooms were staged and the overall quality was very good. Perhaps the highlight was the British Raisers Gold Cup. With the retirement of Koanga Daffodils from this class after fifteen or so victories, and the incentive of a specially donated trophy, an equal record of four entries appeared. Aaron Russ, a young student from Christchurch was the successful exhibitor; probably the youngest person to win an open collection at a National show. His entry was nicely presented and had good flowers of 'Dailmanach', 'Broomhill' and 'Gold Convention' which joined newer introduction 'Goff's Caye' and the seldom seen 'Dunley Hall'. Michael and Marian Brown were a very close second – 'Lennymore' and 'Golden Joy' were nice in their entry, while David Adams came in third. Brogden Bulbs took a good double by adding the South Island NDS Raisers Cup to their North Island success; 'New Hope' and 'Kiwi Ruler' stood out in this section. We thought competition was closer here than in the North with Pleasant Valley's set being a very close second. Their 'Tucaman', 2Y-Y is a lovely bloom, a must for serious growers. While Koanga won all bar one of the classes they entered in the Open Collections, prizes were spread around. Although the only entry, we admired Malroze's winning yellow trumpet set with well-grown blooms of 'Golden Vale' and 'Cameo Sun'. Denise and Neil McQuarrie won the small cups with one of the best entries seen in this class for some time – 'Rockall' (which had a great year), 'Cairntoul' and 'Lynx' were excellent in their group. Michael and Marian Brown won three collection trophies including the white trumpets. 'Temple Splendour', raised by the late David Bell was noted here.

The miniature championship saw a reversal of the North Island results with Colin and Sue Reid making the long trip south worthwhile. David Adams was a close second and Alistair Davey was third of the six quality entrants. The intermediates were well supported and Pleasant Valley's 'Perfeck', 2Y-Y, was almost that and Pleasant Valley's 'Steffi' beat off 18 other entries.

The amateur classes were very strong with new exhibitor Bill Cowie bringing boxes of flowers to swell the entries. Aaron Russ continued his great run by taking home silverware from seven victories. We were most pleased to see Aaron win the amateur class for daffodils raised by exhibitor - an outstanding victory for one so young. He was not able to beat Alistair Davey in the South Island Amateur Championship though. Alistair staged nice vases of 'Centrefold', 'Ebony' and 'Akala' in this entry. Bill Cowie and E & G Hill had a close contest in the amateur threes with the Hills emerging as winners of the Bensemann Trophy for most points. We especially admired their white trumpets which included 'Snowy Morn' and 'Panache'. There were excellent entries in the amateur single blooms with up to 24 in some classes. The doubles had this many with Bill Cowie's 'Fortescue' beating Judy Phimister's 'Spun Honey'. We also noted Ailsa Rollinson winning with 'Radiant Gem' - not her first effort in these classes nor we trust her last. Her brother Garrick also joined the winner's circle with 'Gull'.

The premiers were excellent again. Flowers which were especially good were 'Anitra' (Marian and Michael Brown), 'Xunantunich', 'Moon Shadow' (Denise and Neil McQuarrie), 'Wild Card' 3W-Y but unregistered (Spud Brogden), 'Bandit' (Koanga) and 'Barnesgold' (John and Brenda Byrne).

Two Nelson growers took their first ever Best Blooms - Arch Crerar was thrilled with his 'Cairntoul' which took best amateur as were Kevin and Carol Kerr with their overall Best Bloom 'Polar Sky'. Reserve Best Bloom went to Koanga Daffodils for a Ramsay white double seedling 95:17 ('Kiwi Magic' × 'Springston Charm').

ADS CONVENTION
NIAL WATSON

The National Show and Convention of the American Daffodil Society (ADS) on 18-19 April was hosted by the South West Ohio Daffodil Society (SWODS). It was held across the Ohio River from Cincinnati in Fort Mitchell, Kentucky.

With temperatures unseasonably high there were a surprisingly large number of flowers, and 2,500 blooms were staged in 1,202 entries. Although many showed signs of the hot weather and sun scorch the standard was high.

The guest speaker was Janis Ruksans from Latvia whose illustrated talk on his expeditions into the wilds of Asia in his quest for plant species was extremely interesting. He braved not only inclement natural conditions but also unfriendly border guards and bandits in his quest.

The convention was a great success and a credit to SWODS.

Main Prize Winners

The ADS Challenge Cup for twelve cultivars raised by the exhibitor was won by Brian Duncan with 'Coromandel', 'Ice Dancer' 2W-GWP, 'Lennymore', 'Dorchester', 'Eyrie' 3W-YYP, 'Honeyorange' 2O-R, 'Harbour View' 2W-P, 'Goldfinger', D2100 2Y-P, 'Alto' 2W-P, 'Ring Fence' 3Y-YYR and 'Savoir Faire'. Best Bloom in the Hybridizers section was Nial Watson's 0283 ('Achduart' × 'Ulster Bank').

The Throckmorton Award which requires 15 stems of daffodils each with a different classification (including the colour code) was won by Kathy Walsh. Her flowers were 'Carib Gypsy' 2Y-WWY, 'Spindletop' 3W-Y, 'Hambledon', 'Remembered Kiss' 2W-WWP, 'Swedish Sea' 2Y-Y, 'Modulux' 2W-Y, 'American Dream' 1Y-P, 'Cosmic Dance' 2O-R, 'Samsara', 'Eland', 'Carole Lombard', 'Songket' 2W-GWP, 'Tehidy' 3Y-YYR, 'Ice Wings' and 'Tripartite'. Best Bloom in show 'Carib Gypsy' also came from a vase of three shown by Kathy.

Bill Pannill used several flowers of his own raising in his winning Quinn and Tuggle Award entries. The Harry I Tuggle Jr Trophy calls for twelve cultivars three stems of each. Bill's flowers were 'Savoir Faire', 'Spindletop', 'Noteworthy' 3W-YYO, 'Homestead' 2W-W, 'Lonesome Dove' 2W-W, 'Irvington' 3W-R, 'Spring Break' 2W-P, 'Hurrah' 2Y-Y, 'Monticello' 1W-Y, 'Delta Queen' 2W-P, 'Oregon Pioneer' 2Y-P and 'Tyson's Corner' 3W-GYR. The extremely demanding Carey E Quinn Award calls for 24 cultivars, one stem of each from at least five divisions. Bill's flowers were 'Spindletop', 'Cornell' 3Y-W, 'Tuckahoe' 3W-GYR, 'Notre Dame', 'Affirmation', 'Lone Star' 2W-W, 'Always' 2W-P, 'Rejoice' 3W-GYR, 'Gold Bond', 'Irish Affair', 'Williamsburg' 2W-W, 'Amazing Grace', 'Fortescue' 4W-R, 'Ashland' 2W-Y, 'Page Lee' 3Y-R, 'Cool White' 3W-W, 'Hurrah', 'All American' 2W-R, 'Conestoga', 'Intrigue', 'Explosion' 8Y-O, 'Indian Maid' 7O-R, 'Tyson's Corner' and 89/35/2 2W-WOO ('Urbane' × 'Newport').

The Elise Havens Award for twelve cultivars from divisions 5 to 10 was won by Steve Vinisky, who showed 'Super Seven' 7Y-Y, V93-28 9W-GYR ('Angel Eyes' × poet), 'Art Nouveau' 7W-P, V96-139-5 9W-GYR ('Moyle' × 'Vienna Woods'), V95-120-2 9W-GYR ('Frank's Fancy' × 'Vienna Woods'), 'Chapel Bells' 5Y-Y, V94-60-3 9W-GYR ('Angel Eyes × French poet), V93-72-7 8W-W ('Hillstar' × 'Pango'), V93-16-9 9W-GYR (*N. poeticus* var. *recurvus* × Evans N256). Also included were three 'Hillstar' × *N. triandrus* var. *loiseleurii* seedlings V92-72-16 5W-Y, V92-72-14 5W-Y, and V92-72-11 5W-W the last of which was awarded the Rose Ribbon.

The Roberta C Watrous Award for twelve miniatures, one stem of each, was won by Naomi Liggett with 'Segovia', 'Little Rusky', 'Xit', Galyon 1816N 5Y-Y (*N. fernandesii* × *N. triandrus*), 'Yellow Xit', 'Clare', 'Stafford', 'Hummingbird' 6Y-Y, *N. bulbocodium* subsp. *bulbocodium* var. *graellsii* 13Y-Y, *N. jonquilla* var. *henriquesii* 13Y-Y and *N. bulbocodium* subsp. *bulbocodium* var. *conspicuous*. Best Miniature in show was *N. alpestris* shown by Kathy Anderson.

Display of Miniature Species and Hybrid Narcissi

John Blanchard

In January and February 2001 members of the Daffodil and Tulip Committee paid a couple of visits to the Rock Garden department at Wisley to see species and hybrids of miniature *narcissi*, mostly bulbocodiums, in flower. Members of the Rock Garden Plant Committee joined them. A third visit was made in December 2001. On each occasion we saw a fine collection of *Narcissus* and other "alpine" type plants and we were greatly impressed by the standard of cultivation and the care with which records are kept of the origin of the material. We were able to offer some assistance on naming, but the Bulbocodium Section of *Narcissus* is notoriously difficult and accurate identification is not always possible.

At the Show in the Lawrence Hall on 22-23 January 2002 the wider public had an opportunity to see many of these plants in an exhibit staged by Wisley. A beautifully arranged 4.25m × 3m (14ft × 10ft) island stand contained around 80 pots of bulbocodiums representing a large proportion of the species which are normally in flower at this time of year, together with some bulbocodium hybrids. The species, possibly with one exception, all came from Morocco but a well-presented information board with a map provided a helpful guide to the areas where these and the Spanish and Portuguese species are found in the wild. There was also a good illustrated pamphlet for visitors to take away with them, something that is always appreciated.

Notable among the plants shown were fine clumps of the white *Narcissus romieuxii* subsp. *albidus* and the little-known pale yellow *N. bulbocodium* subsp. *praecox* var. *paucinervis*. There were good pans of *N. romieuxii* showing what a variable species it is (like most) both in shape and colour from almost white through various shades of pale and darker yellow including the selected cultivars 'Atlas Gold', 'Treble Chance' and 'Yellow Pet' with nicely rolled back coronas. Whitest of all was *N. cantabricus* and its subspecies *monophyllus*, though the plants of the latter in the exhibit seemed to have too many leaves for the name to be justified. Hybrids were represented by 'Tarlatan', 'Taffeta' and various representatives of the Nylon Group.

The whole exhibit was well spaced out and dressed with quite large stones that gave it a natural appearance. Possible criticisms were that a few small shrubs or trees might have enhanced the appearance and that it was too high off the ground so that shorter visitors had difficulty in seeing the plants in the centre. If it had been lower they would have been looking down at the flowers more like one does in the wild. A group staged by RHS staff does not qualify for a medal, but the Committee decided that if it had qualified it would have been awarded a Silver Gilt Flora in the Lindley Range. The Rock Garden Department and Gill Skilton in particular must be congratulated on a fine exhibit.

Snowdrops at the RHS February Show

Alan Leslie

For the dedicated galanthophile the RHS London Show in February is rapidly becoming an event not to be missed: not only for the quality of the displays in the Halls and the plants put up for award, but also for the number of fellow addicts who attend, with the consequent opportunity to exchange news about the latest finds. On 19 February 2002 there was the added bonus of an eagerly awaited new snowdrop book to discuss *(Snowdrops : A Monograph of Cultivated* Galanthus by Matt Bishop, Aaron Davis and John Grimshaw, reviewed on page 67).

In the Lawrence Hall Edrom, Broadleigh and Avon Bulbs all had well-grown snowdrops. The Avon Bulbs display included 'Blewbury Tart', Alan Street's 1975 discovery at Blewbury in Oxfordshire. As its flowers face upwards this odd little *nivalis* double flaunts the almost all green inner surfaces of its inner petals full in the face of the observer. Whilst it is certainly no beauty, it has curiosity value. But it was Foxgrove Plants who once again stole the limelight with another splendid and varied display, although even they were showing slight signs of the very early season, which was already making plants in peak condition harder to come by. Their collection of "yellows", which in snowdrop circles have something of a cult following, must have made many deeply envious for these included: 'Lady Elphinstone', 'Sandersii', 'Blonde Inge', 'Ray Cobb', 'Primrose Warburg' and 'Wendy's Gold'. But the plant that stole the Show for many was not on this stand, although it was another yellow snowdrop. It arrived from France that morning with Mark Brown and is the first *G. nivalis* to have both a yellow ovary, yellow inner petal marking plus a distinct V-shaped yellow mark on the *outside* of the outer petals. This was completely new and distinct and went immediately to the top of everyone's list of desiderata. The lucky man found three flowering clumps amongst a host of normal *nivalis* in a garden in Normandy. It is to be called 'Ecusson d'Or'.

Upstairs the Joint Rock Garden Plant Committee were again treated to a trio of impeccably presented snowdrops from Dr Ronald Mackenzie. Of these 'Cowhouse Green' caught their eye as a distinct cultivar and received an emphatic Award of Merit on its first outing. This is a *nivalis* × *plicatus* derivative discovered by Mark Brown, in the late 1980s, in a Buckinghamshire garden. Each flower has green veins on the apical half of the outer side of the outer petals the veins connected by a green wash, whilst the inner petals sport a dark green, apical, W-shaped marking, the outer arms of which continue as a diffuse line up the side of the petals to join the pale green marking at the base. Reputedly a tricky plant to grow well but repaying the effort, not to mention the expense.

Dr Mackenzie's two other snowdrops were both of considerable interest but did not move the judges into award mode. *G. krasnovii* has probably never been exhibited before, as this montane species from western Georgia and north-east Turkey was only described in 1963 and although known in cultivation for a limited period is already marked as a "difficult" plant to grow (not that many have had a chance to try). The broad, convolute, green (not glaucous) leaves and the long-clawed outer segments combined with the very unusual pointed tips to the inner petals make this a highly distinctive taxon. The third in the trio was the Baytop collection no. 34474 attributed to *G. rizehensis*, which provoked considerable discussion as the habit, colour and vernation of the leaves did not seem to match other cultivated plants of this species. This vigorous, broad-leaved clone is now known to be a triploid and it seems that in gardens experience of this species has been confined to too limited a range of material.

Evidence of three other significant finds became apparent during the day. Most tantalising of these was a set of colour prints brought over to the Show from Dresden by Jörg Lebsa, taken in a locality in southern Turkey (See Jörg Lebsa's article on page 61). These showed an extensive population of a single-spotted, grey-leaved convolute snowdrop (*G. elwesii* var. *monostictus*, perhaps) in which a significant number of plants were virescent: with inner petal markings extended partially or completely over the outer surface of the petal and combined with various green markings on the outside of the outers: some of the latter just in the form of a small dot of green, others as a short line, but all sorts of variants were occurring. Combine all this with a November flowering season and the potential for a whole new set of cultivars is soon evident. The botanical relationships of this population would probably also repay further study.

Just as startling as this was the report from another visitor to the Show (P H White) of a first-class poculiform plicate snowdrop. The only two previous reports of such plants have not resulted in much success in their cultivation, so this new garden find, of just a few plants on the edge of a clump of what is thought to be G. *plicatus* subsp. *byzantinus*, will be watched with eager anticipation. There are no inner markings on the elongated inner segments, the outers are broadly rounded and the plants overall stature is short. It has not yet been named.

Last but by no means least was yet another new poculiform snowdrop, exhibited by Richard Nutt in his buttonhole! This one had been named as *G.* 'Henry's white Lady' and is a particularly fine example of a poculiform *nivalis*. The Henry concerned is Henry Plumbridge an ex policeman and former neighbour of Mr Nutt, for whom he used to mow the lawns. Mr Plumbridge found it in an old garden, with other more typical *G. nivalis*. Mr Nutt reports that unlike similar plants such as 'Sandhill Gate' it is a good grower and it was certainly to be coveted as seen!

As interest in snowdrops continues to grow and more people look closely at populations in the wild and in cultivation we can expect more exciting finds to be reported in the future; the variations familiar in the best known snowdrop G. *nivalis* are slowly but surely being unearthed in other species.

Acknowledgements
My thanks are due to Mark Brown, Alan Street, Matt Bishop, Ruby Baker and Richard Nutt for information contained in this note.

RHS Early Daffodil Competition

John Goddard

Advocates of global warming certainly had something to shout about this year. The mild, wet winter advanced flowering by about two or three weeks in the Midlands and South East resulting in 271 stems being staged by about twelve exhibitors at this normally very small show on 12-13 March.

Collection Classes

The class for six cultivars from any division, one stem of each, was won again by John Gibson with his own seedlings, all with a yellow perianth. His G-001 1Y-O was really outstanding, and was awarded Best Bloom and Best Unregistered Seedling in show. Raised from 'Golden Vale' × 'Corbiere' G-001 has a pale orange trumpet and excellent form and has since been named 'Eastbrook Sunrise' (see Fig. 5). Ron Scamp was second with a very good set which included 'Isambard' 4Y-R and S380 2Y-YYO, a flower which just misses trumpet measurements. John Parkinson had a neat collection in third place, including 'Goldfinger', which usually blooms a month later.

There were only two entries in the class for three vases of three blooms from any division or divisions. John Gibson just got home in first place and I thought that 'Predator' 1W-Y was his best bloom. Ron Scamp had a very fine 'Heamoor' 4Y-O in his set. This cultivar is emerging as one to grow for early shows.

Four entries in the class for three vases of division 6 cultivars, three blooms of each filled out the show-bench rather nicely. I benefited from the early season to win with 'Lemon Silk' 6YYW-W, 'Trena' 6W-Y and 'Rapture' 6Y-Y. These overseas cultivars seem to have eclipsed the older varieties now. Whatever happened to 'Dove Wings'? Ron Scamp was the bridesmaid again here, but showed a nice example of 'Peppercorn' 6YYW-YW one of his raisings which was new to me. Janine Doulton was third but had a cracking vase of 'Trena' in her exhibit.

Seven blooms from division 6 are hard to find but at last Ron Scamp managed to win first place with superb 'Rapture'. Janine was second with a mixed vase which included her good stock of 'Trena' and 'Lemon Silk'. Steve Holden weighed in with more 'Rapture' What a super cultivar this is now that it has settled down to our climate.

Single Bloom Classes

Classes 5 and 6 drew ten entries each which must be a record for the Early Show. John Gibson produced his G001 again to win the trumpets although he was run close by Steve Holden with an outstanding 'Beaulieu' 1Y-Y and Ron Scamp's 'Saint Budock' 1Y-Y which was large for the cultivar. Large cups were strongly supported and Steve Holden produced a lovely 'Broadway Village' 2Y-YRR which is a banker for southern growers. Clive Postles says that this was his first registered seedling of his own raising in 1985 and is justly proud that it has proved to be so successful. John Gibson's 'Goldhanger' 2Y-Y and Eddie Jarman's 2Y-R seedling 728 were second and third respectively. Ron Scamp's 'New Life' 3W-W was well worth first prize despite being the only entry in division 3.

The division 6 classes were well supported with 'Rapture' and 'Trena' dominant. My 'Rapture' was judged to be ahead of the rest but

Hofflands Daffodils

Suppliers of Quality Daffodil Bulbs to the World

Raisers of Many Top Prize-winning Varieties

R.H.S. Gold Medal 1995, 1998 & 1999

A.D.S. Trophy 1996 & 1997

Engleheart Cup 1995

Send for our free catalogue

JOHN & ROSEMARY PEARSON
Hofflands, Little Totham Road, Goldhanger,
Maldon, Essex. CM9 8AP. U. K.
E-Mail: Hofflands@care4free.net
Telephone: (44) (0)1621 788678
Fax: (44) (0)1621 788445

Ron Scamp sneaked into second place with seedling S559; neat but not fully reflexed in the perianth. Janine Doulton beat me in the 'Trena' class, but it was all very close.

The class for one stem from any other division used to be a lost cause in the old days, but now we have split coronas and early jonquils to choose from. Ron Scamp showed a huge 'Jack Wood' 11aY-O to beat Reg Nicholl's three-headed 'Marzo' 7Y-Y. Reg was unlucky here as this was the first triple header that most of us had seen of this cultivar; and fresh too!

The class for an unregistered seedling raised by the exhibitor produced eleven entries Eddie Jarman was first and second here with yellow-red seedlings 728 and 561. The judges are certainly partial to yellow-reds because John Gibson's 3-6-89 2Y-R came in third. Ron Scamp's unplaced S56-86-1 4W-Y showed promise.

Miniatures

The class for three vases of three miniatures was won by Ron Scamp and produced the Best Miniature and Reserve Best Bloom in show with one of the stems of 'Dandubar' (see Fig. 7). Raised from *N. jonquilla* var. *henriquesii* × *N. scaberulus* by Jane Petersfield of Sittingbourne in Kent, 'Dandubar' is a promising result from what I am told is an unusual breeding programme. John Blanchard was the only entrant in the two classes for miniatures raised by the exhibitor; I did like his 'Pequenita' 7Y-Y. He also won the classes for miniature species or wild hybrids from division 13 with *N. intermedius, N. aureus,* and *N. incurvicervicus* and *N. cordubensis* respectively. I liked Janine Doulton's 'Elka' and her three headed old-favourite 'Tête-à-Tête'. Ron Scamp came up with a lovely 'Picoblanco' and *N. odoratus* to show his versatility. Both John Gibson and John Parkinson are also prominent growers of miniatures and won with *N. bulbocodium* var. *citrinus* and *N. ochroleucus* respectively.

Novices

A field day here for Peter Mazillus who won four first and a second prize. His best flower was 'Surfside' 6W-Y and he looks likely to become a serious exhibitor at future shows.

So here we saw one of the best Early Competitions in this the Golden Jubilee Year.

Tulips

Experienced visitors to the Lawrence Hall always go upstairs to the front of the hall to look at the interesting and often rare plants which have seen by RHS Committees. On this occasion the Director of the Royal Botanic Gardens at Kew had shown a superb pot of a form of *T. sylvestris* subsp. *australis* to the Daffodil and Tulip Committee (see Fig. 11). This Tunisian collection required the protection of a frame and was unusual in the green (not reddish) back to the petals and the handsome decumbent grey-green foliage.

RESULTS
PETER WILKINS

The number in brackets denotes the number of entries staged in the class

Standard and Intermediate Daffodils

Class 1: Six cultivars, any division or divisions, one bloom of each. (4). 1. J Gibson: G.001 (1Y-O) (Best Bloom in show), 1-20-92 (2Y-Y), 3-6-89 (2Y-R), 2-20-92 (2Y-Y), A6-91 (1Y-Y), C6-91 (1Y-Y). 2 R A Scamp: Helford Dawn, Isambard, 525-92-1 (1Y-Y), S830 (2Y-Y), S46-25-1 (4Y-Y), Jack Wood. 3. J M Parkinson: Pink Silk, Goldfinger, 94-2 (1Y-Y), Goffs Caye, Nederburg, Mulroy Bay. 4. E Jarman: 728 (2Y-R), 446 (1W-W), 596 (1Y-W), 580 (2O-R), 257 (4Y-R), 576 (2Y-R).

Class 2: Three cultivars, any division or divisions, three blooms of each. (2). 1. J Gibson: Michaels Gold, Predator, Golden Joy. 2. R A Scamp: Hero, Heamoor, Dimity.

Class 3: Three cultivars, division 6, three blooms of each. (4). 1. J Goddard: Lemon Silk, Trena, Rapture. 2. R A Scamp: Peppercorn, The Alliance, Trena. 3. Mrs J Doulton: Warbler, Trena, Emperor's Waltz.

Class 4: Seven Blooms, division 6, one or more cultivars. (5). 1. R A Scamp: Rapture 2. Mrs J Doulton: Lemon Silk, Rapture, Warbler, Swift Arrow. 3. S Holden: Rapture.

Class 5: One Cultivar, Division 1, one bloom. (10). 1. J Gibson: G001, 2. S Holden: Beaulieu. 3. R A Scamp: St Budock.
Class 6: One Cultivar, Division 2, one bloom. (4). 1. S Holden: Broadway Village. 2. J Gibson: Goldhanger. 3. E Jarman: 728 (2Y-R).
Class 7: One Cultivar, Division 3, one bloom. (1). 1. R A Scamp: New Life.
Class 8: One Cultivar, Division 4, one bloom. (5). 1. S Holden: Sussex Bonfire, 2. J Goddard: Heamoor. 3. R A Scamp: Kiwi Sunset.
Class 9: One Cultivar, Division 6, yellow perianth, one bloom. (11). 1. J Goddard: Rapture. 2. R A Scamp: S559 (6Y-Y). 3. S Holden: Rapture.
Class 10: One Cultivar, Division 6, white perianth, one bloom. (7). 1. Mrs J Doulton: Trena. 2. J Goddard: Trena. 3. S Holden: Trena.
Class 11: One Cultivar, Any Other Division, one bloom. (6). 1. R A Scamp: Jack Wood. 2. R Nicholl: Marzo. 3. R Wiseman: Avalanche.
Class 12: One Intermediate Cultivar from Divisions 1 to 4, one bloom. (2). 1. J M Parkinson: 91-11 (2W-P). 2. R A Scamp: Salakee.
Class 13: One Unregistered Cultivar, bred and raised by the Exhibitor, one bloom. (11). 1. E Jarman: 728 (2Y-R). 2. E Jarman: 561 (2Y-R). 3. J Gibson: 3-6-89 (2Y-R).

Miniature and Wild Daffodils
Class 14: Three Miniature Cultivars, bred and raised by the Exhibitor, one bloom of each. (1). 1. J W Blanchard: Shillingstone, 94/4A (*N. atlanticus* × *N. asturiensis*), Pequenita.
Class 15: One Miniature Cultivar, bred and raised by the Exhibitor, one bloom. (1) . 1. J W Blanchard: 63/2B (*N. watieri* × *N calcicola*).
Class 16: Three Miniature Cultivars, three blooms of each. (3). 1. R A Scamp: Canaliculatus, Dandubar (Best Miniature, Reserve Best Bloom in show), Picoblanco. 2. R Wiseman: Midget, Smarple, Little Gem.
Class 17: Three Miniature Species or Wild hybrids from Division 13, three blooms of each. (2). 1. J W Blanchard: *N. aureus*, *N.* × *intermedius*, *N.* × *incurvicervicus*. 2. J Gibson: *N. bulbocodium* var. *citrinus*, *N. hedraeanthus* var. *luteolentus*, *N. assoanus*.
Class 18: One Miniature Cultivar, three bloom. (5). 1. J Gibson: Midget, 2. Mrs J Doulton: Elka, 3. R A Scamp: Picoblanco.
Class 19: One Miniature Species or Wild hybrid from Division 13, three blooms. (3). 1. J W Blanchard: *N. cordubensis*. 2. R A Scamp: *N. odoratus*. 3. J M Parkinson: *N. jonquilla henriquesii*.
Classes 20: One Miniature Cultivar (excluding Division 10), one bloom. (6). 1. Mrs J Doulton: Tête-à-Tête. 2. J W Blanchard: 63/2B (*N. watieri* × *N. calcicola*). 3. Minnow.
Class 21: One Miniature Species or Wild hybrid from Division 13 (excluding the Bulbocodium section), one bloom. (6) 1. R Nicholl: *N. ubriquensis*. 2. R A Scamp: *N. odoratus*. 3. Mrs J Doulton: *N. cordubensis*
Class 22: One Cultivar from Division 10, or one Species or Wild Hybrid from the Bulbocodium section of Division 13, one bloom. (5). 1. J Gibson: *N. bulbocodium* var. *citrinus*. 2. J M Parkinson: *N. bulbocodium conspicuus*. 3. R Sampson: *N. bulbocodium conspicuus*.
Class 23: One Species or Wild Hybrid from Division 13 (other than miniature), one bloom. (4). 1. J M Parkinson: *N. tazetta ochroleucus*. 2. J W Blanchard: *N. varduliensis*. 3. R Wiseman: *N. moschatus*.

Novice Classes
Class 24: One cultivar, Division 1, one bloom. (1). 1. P Mazillus: Spellbinder.
Class 25: One cultivar, Division 2, one bloom. (1) 2. P Mazillus: Fragrant Breeze.
Class 26: One cultivar, Division 3, one bloom. (0)
Class 27: One cultivar, Division 4, one bloom. (1) 1. P Mazillus: Golden Ducat.
Class 28: One cultivar, Division 6, yellow perianth, one bloom. (2). 1. P Mazillus: February Gold. 2. Mrs D Skudder: Jetfire.
Class 29: One cultivar, Division 6, white perianth, one bloom. (1). 1. P Mazillus: Surfside.
Class 30: One cultivar, Any other Division, one bloom. (1). No award.

RHS Daffodil Show

Reg Nicholl

The cancellation of the Daffodil show in deference to the passing of the Queen Mother meant that the Late Competition due to be held on 23-24 April took on the mantle of the former. Unfortunately, as the season was very early this year, many exhibitors were short of flowers. There were only 432 stems on display and for the second time in recent years there were no trade stands to appreciate.

Seedling classes

However, there were good flowers to be seen and those making up both entries in the Engleheart Cup, requiring twelve blooms raised by the exhibitor, produced some of them. Brian Duncan was the winner and his display included the Best Bloom in the show 'Dorchester' 4W-P. Brian's exemplary collection also included the Best Bloom division 3 'Jake' 3Y-GOO and one other of excellent form, seedling 2108 ('Clouds Rest' × 'June Lake') which is shown on the front cover and featured a very smooth perianth with a startling almost red cup. Ron Scamp was runner up and staged a record five doubles in his group, one of which S739 was a delightful all-white flower of beautiful form.

The single entry in the class for six seedlings raised by the exhibitor belonged to Eddie Jarman and featured an extremely smooth 3W-W bloom 544 and an unusually heavily petalled double 818 which could best be described as peaches and cream! Only one entry too in the three seedling class, from Peter Mills, but worth a mention for an outstanding 3O-R flower numbered 92/17A that was richly hued.

British breeders are now producing some imposing split-corona flowers exemplified by those staged in the three seedling class. Two unnamed seedlings with superb white perianths and pink/white coronas, 1734 and 1875, together with his terracotta centred 'Electrus' 11aW-GPP gave Brian Duncan pride of place just ahead of Ron Scamp whose all yellow 'Pampaluna' 11aY-Y was really first class.

Intermediate daffodils are now receiving more attention from the breeders and the four entries were all of merit. First was Eddie Jarman with an almost circular flower 840, with a broad white perianth complementing a mostly yellow corona with a pink rim, followed by Ron Scamp's delightful all-yellow double S816. Peter Mills took third place with a really smooth 2W-W 90/21-9.

Open classes

The collection classes were the hardest hit in the show with but a single entry in the nine. John Goddard was the sole exhibitor and his fine selection in the class for six cultivars raised outside Europe featured a splendid bloom of the American raised 'Gull' 2W-W.

Single bloom classes

The Single Bloom classes started with a fine win for Brian Duncan whose 'Goldfinger' 1Y-Y narrowly beat David Matthews' 'Sperrin Gold'. Dennis Marshall came third with 'Hadlow Down'. However Best Bloom in division 1 was David Matthews' magnificent 'Fresh Lime' 1YYW-Y with other reversed bicolour seedlings of Eddie Jarman 305, and Ron Scamp S718 following on. An outstanding pink trumpet with yellow perianth, labelled 2078 was another of Brian Duncan's winning seedlings. Bred from an Anglo-American cross 'Filoli' × 'Lorikeet', 2078 just pipped David Matthews' 'American Shores' 1Y-P. However David staged a splendid 'Panache' in the all-white class, the like of which had not been seen for many years.

'White Star' and 'Silent Valley' took the remaining places for Pam Cox and Ron Sampson respectively.

Division 2 exhibits were better supported and in the all-yellow class Dennis Marshall produced a grand bloom of 'Whisky Mac' to win (see Fig. 9). David Matthews staged a fine 'Clouded Yellow' 2YYW-Y and Brian Duncan seedling 2113, an elegant 'Burning Bush' × 'Gold Bond' cross took the final place.

Unusually, an unknown flower which looked remarkably like 'State Express' 2Y-GOO took the honours for David Matthews. It beat a neat Eddie Jarman seedling 839 and left John Goddard with his home town cultivar 'Banstead Village' third.

The use of 'Gold Bond' 2Y-Y in its parentage, this time with 'Triple Crown' 3W-GYR gave Brian Duncan's seedling 2075 first just to the fore of Pam Cox's colourful 'Shangani' 2Y-YYR. Pam was to claim prime place and Best Bloom division 2 with an imposing flower of the certainty for its class 'Altun Ha'! With flowers of the same cultivar Eddie Jarman and David Matthews were in the minor positions.

John Goddard staged an excellent flower of the unusually coloured 'Honeybourne' 2W-Y, just ahead of Janine Doulton's 'Soft Focus' with Eddie Jarman third with another good seedling 705, of bright colour contrast.

Brian Duncan's first prize winner, 1913, in class 139 was an engaging 2W-GWR raised from the crossing of two pink cultivars. 'Royal Marine' 2W-YOO gave second place to David Matthews with Malcolm Bradbury in final position with the Bill Bender raised 'Conestoga' 2W-GYO.

The best-supported class in the show was the 2W-Ps with eleven entries, which was won by Ian Erskine with 'Fragrant Rose' 2W-GPP. This bloom was grown in Dublin, exhibited in Belfast, where it was Best Bloom in the show on the Saturday before London; returned to Dublin and thence to Westminster. Full marks to Ian for enterprise and endeavour. Dennis Marshall's 'Cape Point' 2W-P came second followed by Eddie Jarman's nicely contrasted seedling 93.41.2. Conversely in the class for pink-rimmed cultivars Eddie's seedling 826 out pointed Denis's 'June Lake', with Brian Duncan's 'Savoir Faire' completing the trio.

The all-white division 2 class is often the best supported but here we had just eight entries. Nevertheless John Goddard staged a majestic 'Sheelagh Rowan' to capture the number one spot. Second was V and G Ellams' nice 'Ashmore' with the rarely seen 'Inverpolly' from Dennis Marshall third. David Matthews also had a fine unplaced 'Sheelagh Rowan'.

The Australian raised 'Nonchalant' 3Y-Y is now finding a regular place on the show bench and took two of the three places. Frank Verge and John Smith exhibiting it were separated by an unnamed Clive Postles seedling shown by David Matthews.

'Jake' 3Y-GOO has now become the benchmark flower in its class and Eddie Jarman produced a magnificent specimen with David Matthews close behind with more of the same. Third was Barry Ridsdale choosing to show 'Stanway' 3Y-ORR. In the succeeding rimmed class Brian Duncan with his oddly named 'Ring Fence' 3Y-YYR was first ahead of Ron Scamp's 'Tiffany Jade' 3Y-YYR with John Smith's 'Badbury Rings' 3Y-YYR third.

A Peter Mills seedling, 91-49C-2, was first in the all-orange division 3 class but its colouring was somewhat indeterminate. Nevertheless the judges preferred it to the two flowers of 'Brodick' shown by Messrs Duncan and Matthews.

Rather surprisingly an excellent bloom of the infrequently seen 'Cedar Hills' 3W-GYY outpaced 'Evesham' and 'Moon Shadow'. Relative old-timers 'Cairntoul' and 'Doctor Hugh' took the leading two places for Frank Verge and Pam Cox respectively with the newer 'Cavalryman' 3W-R of Brian Duncan making the final place. 'Carole Lombard' 3W-YYO like its namesake a beautiful face, led for Pam Cox and Ron Scamp but Eddie Jarman's pretty seedling 773 might have fared better.

Small cupped flowers with pink coronas and white perianths have been a long time coming from breeders but Brian Duncan has certainly raised a fine example with seedling 2106, which has a superb deep pink, almost red, rim to the corona.

The all-white class was dominated by 'Cool Crystal' but on this occasion Dennis Marshall and Frank Verge's flowers were separated by another first class Eddie Jarman seedling 544 which must surely be named. The classes for doubles averaged half a dozen entries each and in the all-yellow one David Matthews 'Spun Honey' won from the down-under 'Tasgem'. Barry Ridsdale and John Smith both staged 'Manly' in the next class but were separated by Ron Scamp with his own 'Poppy's Choice', a flower that seems to have been overlooked by exhibitors given its pleasing appearance. Another of his raisings S740 was close behind John Smith's fine 'Atholl Palace' 4W-Y in the following class completed by the cultivar 'Unique' shown by John Goddard.

'Dorchester' is so outstanding in the pink class that it is almost unbeatable because of its superb form and its raiser Brian Duncan produced another excellent bloom to win the class again. Denis Marshall also staged one but the rot was stopped metaphorically speaking by another superior seedling from Eddie Jarman 337. Like Dochester, 'Gay Kybo' is the one to conquer in its colour class and cleared the board for Messrs Goddard, Scamp and Smith.

Higher divisions

The triandrus section produced just ten flowers the best of them being Ron Scamp's stem of 'Fairy Chimes', rather better than the cyclamineus section which could only muster eight flowers the best of which was Brian Duncan's own 'Elizabeth Ann'.

Division 7 provided us with another of Ron Scamp's excellent raisings S729 in the all yellow class, which was accorded the Best Bloom, just beating another of his raising 'Boscastle' shown by Pam Cox. The remaining five 'Stratosphere' staged were ignored by the judges as not being colour compliant which raised an eyebrow or two. This cultivar found favour in the following class being staged by Dennis Marshall and Geoff Ridley but even in this class they only took the minor placings behind Pam Cox's 'Mowser'. 'Ladies' Choice' is now emerging as a winner in a thinly populated class for all-white flowers and gave Dennis Marshall and Pam Cox prime places with third going to 'St Piran'.

Dennis Marshall was really out on his own with the single stem from division 8, 'Silver Chimes'.

Ron Scamp was very much to the fore again with an exceptionally smooth seedling S1035, to win not only the Poeticus class but the Best Bloom division 9 as well. His other raising 'Blisland' shown by Michael Bird was runner up. For some reason judges tend not to care overmuch for 'Killearnan' but it was a neat flower that gave John Smith final place.

Most split-corona daffodils raised in recent years, have been of the collar type, 11a, and it is something of a rarity if a papillon cultivar, 11b appears on the show bench. One such was Brian Duncan's seedling 1736 which was subsequently named 'Jodi' (see Fig. 8). 'Jodi' was a really outstanding flower with a very smooth perianth of thick texture surmounted by a pink and white corona of very even displacement. Not only was it chosen as Best Bloom in its division but it was also selected as Best Unregistered Seedling in the show.

Amateur classes

The major class for amateurs, requiring 15 vases of 3 blooms was not contested and the Richardson Trophy for twelve cultivars representing divisions 1 to 4 saw David Matthews as the sole entrant. Certainly he would have welcomed some competition but staged a fine collection which include an excellent 'Crowndale' and a rather captivating bloom of 'Little Polly' 3Y-R.

Novice section

Derrick Turbitt came over from Portstewart to find himself winning all before him in the Novice Classes and staging a first class flower of 'Misty Glen' as Best bloom in the section.

On reflection this was not a show of the highest quality or greatest quantity but perhaps best remembered for the number of excellent seedlings which were displayed and the fact that only 25 exhibitors were, in a very difficult season, able to find flowers of sufficient merit to grace the show bench. Next year sees the wholly new venture when the Daffodil Show moves to the newly furbished Hillside Events Centre at Wisley.

RESULTS
Peter Wilkins

The number in brackets denotes the number of entries staged in the class

SECTION 1 – OPEN CLASSES

Class 101: Twelve cultivars, bred and raised by the exhibitor, one bloom of each. (2) 1. B S Duncan: Dorchester (Best Bloom in show, Best Bloom Division 4), 1903 (2Y-R), Cape Point, Gold Bond, Outline, 2559 (2W-WWP), Skywalker, 2118 (3W-Y), Alto, Honeyorange, 2108 (2W-R), Jake. 2. R A Scamp: Rebekah, Poppy's Choice, S739 (4W-W), S718 (1Y-W), S725 (3W-WR), S740 (4W-W), Pampaluna, S691 (4W-P), S649 (3W-Y), Littlefield, S939 (9W-O), S734 (7Y-Y).

Class 102: Six cultivars, bred and raised by the exhibitor, one bloom of each. (1) 1. E Jarman: 520 (2W-W), 93-41-2 (2W-P), 337 (4W-P), 544 (3W-W), 828 (2W-P), 818 (4W-P).

Class 103: Three cultivars, bred and raised by the exhibitor, one bloom of each. (1) 1. P Mills: 92/17-A (2O-R), 90/17B-4 (2W-W), 87/42-2 (2Y-W).

Class 104: Three cultivars from any of divisions 5 to 10 and 12, bred and raised by the exhibitor, one bloom of each. (2) 1. R A Scamp: Blisland, Littlefield, S734 (7Y-Y). 2. B S Duncan: Elizabeth Anne, Lilac Charm, Ladies Choice.

Class 105: Three cultivars from Division 11, bred and raised by the exhibitor, one bloom of each. (2) 1. B S Duncan: 1875 (11aW-YP), 1734 (11aW-P), Electrus. 2. R A Scamp: Carnyorth, Menehay, Panpaluna.

Class 106: One intermediate cultivar from Divisions 1 to 4, bred and raised by the exhibitor, one bloom. (4) 1. E Jarman: 840 (2W-YYP). 2. R A Scamp: S816 (4Y-Y). 3. P Mills: 90/21-9 (2W-W).

Class 107: Three Miniature Cultivars, bred and raised by the exhibitor, one bloom of each (0)

Class 108: One Miniature Cultivar, bred and raised by the exhibitor, one bloom (1) 1. J W Blanchard: Crevette.

Class 109: Six Cultivars of White Daffodils from one or more of divisions 1 to 3, three blooms of each. (0)

Class 110: Three Cultivars from one or more of divisions 1 to 3, three blooms of each. (0)

Class 111: Three Cultivars, Division 4, three blooms of each. (0).

Class 112: Three Cultivars from any of Divisions 5 to 10 and 12, three blooms of each. (0)

Class 113: Three Cultivars, Division 11, three blooms of each. (0)

Class 114: Three Cultivars from one or more of Divisions 1 to 3, with pink colouring in the corona, three blooms of each. (0)

Class 115: Three Cultivars not in commerce, from any Division or Divisions, three blooms of each. (0)

Class 116: Seven blooms, Division 1, one or more cultivars. (0)

Class 117: Six Cultivars raised outside the continent of Europe, any Division or Divisions., one bloom of each. (1) 1. J Goddard: Cool Crystal, Gull, Yum Yum, Oakland, Proska, Silent Pink.

Class 118: Twelve Cultivars, representing each of divisions 1 to 4, one bloom of each. (Horticultural Societies' Collection). (0)

Class 119: One Intermediate Cultivar from Division 1 to 4, three blooms (2) 1. B S Duncan: Lauren. 2. Mrs P Cox: Signorina.

Class 120: Three Miniature Species or Wild Hybrids from Division 13, three blooms of each. (0)

Class 121: Three Miniature Cultivars, three blooms of each. (2) 1. R Sampson: Hawera (Best Miniature), Pixies Sister, Sun Disc. 2. R A Scamp: Baby Moon, Segovia, Sun Disc.

Class 122: One Miniature Species or Wild Hybrid from Division 13, three blooms. (3) 1. R A Scamp: *N. jonquilla*. 2. J W Blanchard: *N. bulbocodium citrinus*. 3. R Sampson: *N. poeticus hellenicus*.

Class 123: One Miniature Cultivar, three blooms. (3) 1. R A Scamp: Fairy Chimes. 2. Mrs P Cox: Sun Disc. 3. M Bradbury: Segovia.

Class 124: One bloom Division 1, Perianth yellow, Corona yellow. (7) 1. B S Duncan: Goldfinger. 2. D Matthews: Sperrin Gold. 3. Mr & Mrs D Marshall: Hadlow Down.

Class 125: One bloom Division 1, Perianth yellow, Corona Orange or Red (0)

Class 126: One bloom Division 1, Perianth yellow, Corona White, with or without a yellow rim. (4) 1. D

Matthews: Fresh Lime (Best Bloom Division 1) 2. E Jarman: 305. 3. R A Scamp: S718

Class 127: One bloom Division 1, Perianth yellow, Corona in any other colour or colour combination. (2) 1. B S Duncan: 2078 (1Y-P), 2. D Matthews: American Shores.

Class 128: One bloom Division 1, Perianth white, Corona Yellow or White and Yellow. (1) B S Duncan: Queens Guard.

Class 129: One bloom Division 1, Perianth white, Corona White (5) 1. D Matthews: Panache. 2. Mrs P Cox: White Star. 3. R Sampson: Silent Valley.

Class 130: One bloom Division 1, Perianth white, Corona in any other colour or colour combination. (2) 1. J Goddard: Korora Bay. 2. B S Duncan: Chanson.

Class 131: One bloom Division 1, Perianth any Colour or Colours, Corona any colour. Cultivar not eligible for classes 124 to 130 inclusive. (1) 1. B S Duncan: Edenderry.

Class 132: One bloom Division 2, Perianth Yellow, Corona Yellow. (6) 1. Mr & Mrs D Marshall: Whisky Mac. 2. D Matthews: Clouded Yellow. 3. B S Duncan: 2113.

Class 133: One bloom Division 2, Perianth Yellow, Corona Orange or Red. (6) 1. D Matthews: unknown. 2. E Jarman: 839. 3. J Goddard: Banstead Village.

Class 134: One bloom Division 2, Perianth Yellow, Corona with Orange or Red rim. (2) 1. B S Duncan: 2075. 3. Mrs P Cox: Shangani.

Class 135: One bloom Division 2, Perianth Yellow, Corona containing Pink. (5) 1. B S Duncan: Pink Perry. 2. D Matthews: New Dawn. 3. M Bird: Sandy Cove.

Class 136: One bloom Division 2, Perianth Yellow, Corona white, with or without a yellow rim. (6). 1. Mrs P Cox: Altun Ha. (Best Bloom Division 2). 2. E Jarman: Altun Ha. 3. D Matthews: Altun Ha.

Class 137: One bloom Division 2, Perianth Orange, Corona Orange or Red. (1) 1. B S Duncan: Dawn Run.

Class 138: One bloom Division 2, Perianth White, Corona Yellow or White & Yellow. (7) 1. J Goddard: Honeybourne. 2. Mrs J Doulton: Soft Focus. 3. E Jarman: 705.

Class 139: One bloom Division 2, Perianth White, Corona Orange or Red. (6) 1. B S Duncan: 1913. 2. D Matthews: Royal Marine. 3. M Bradbury: Conestoga.

Class 140: One bloom Division 2, Perianth White, Corona with Orange or Red rim. (2) 2. P Mills 92/24-14. 3. R A Scamp: Calamansack.

Class 141: One bloom Division 2, Perianth White, Corona Pink. (11) 1. I Erskine: Fragrant Rose. 2. Mr & Mrs D Marshall: Cape Point. 3. E Jarman: 93-41-2

Class 142: One bloom Division 2, Perianth White, Corona with Pink rim. (10) 1. E Jarman: 826. 2. Mr & Mrs D Marshall: June Lake. 3. B S Duncan: Savoire Faire.

Class 143: One bloom Division 2, Perianth White, Corona White. (8) 1. J Goddard: Sheelagh Rowan. 2. V & G Ellam: Ashmore. 3. Mr & Mrs D Marshall: Inverpolly.

Class 144: One bloom Division 2, Perianth any colour or colours, Corona any colour, Cultivar not eligible for classes 132 to 143 inclusive. (0)

Class 145: One bloom Division 3, Perianth Yellow, Corona Yellow. (5) 1. F Verge: Nonchalant. 2. D Matthews: Postles seedling. 3. J H Smith: Nonchalant.

Class 146: One bloom Division 3, Perianth Yellow, Corona Orange or Red. (8) 1. E Jarman: Jake. 2. D Matthews: Jake. 3. B Ridsdale: Stanway.

Class 147: One bloom Division 3, Perianth Yellow, Corona with Orange or Red rim. (7) 1. B S Duncan: Ring Fence. 2. R A Scamp: Tiffany Jade. 3. J H Smith: Badbury Rings.

Class 148: One bloom Division 3, Perianth Yellow, Corona White, with or without a yellow rim. (0).

Class 149: One bloom Division 3, Perianth Orange, Corona Orange or Red. (4) 1. P Mills: 91/49C-2. 2. B S Duncan: Brodick. 3. D Matthews: Brodick.

Class 150: One bloom Division 3, Perianth White, Corona Yellow or White and Yellow. (5) 1. R A Scamp: Cedar Hill. 2. D Matthews: Evesham. 3. F Verge: Moon Shadow.

Class 151: One bloom Division 3, Perianth White, Corona Orange or Red. (4) 1. F Verge: Cairntoul. 2. Mrs P Cox: Dr Hugh. 3. B S Duncan: Cavalryman.

Class 152: One bloom Division 3, Perianth White, Corona with Orange or Red rim. (5). 1. Mrs P Cox: Carole Lombard. 2. R A Scamp: Carole Lombard. 3. E Jarman: 773.

Class 153: One bloom Division 3, Perianth White, Corona containing Pink. (1) 1.B S Duncan: 2106.

Class 154: One bloom Division 3, Perianth White, Corona White. (9) 1. Mr & Mrs D Marshall: Cool Crystal. 2. E Jarman: 544. 3. F Verge: Cool Crystal.

Class 155: One bloom Division 3, Perianth any colour or colours, Corona any colour, Cultivar not eligible for classes 145 to 154 inclusive. (0)

Class 156: One bloom Division 4, Perianth and petaloids segments - Yellow, corona segments Yellow. (6) 1. D Matthews: Spun Honey. 2. J H Smith: Tasgem. 3. M Bird: Marjorie Treveal.

Class 157: One bloom Division 4, Perianth and petaloids segments - Yellow, corona segments Orange or Red. (4) 1. B Ridsdale: Manley. 2. R A Scamp: Poppy's Choice. 3. J H Smith: Manley.

Class 158: One bloom Division 4, Perianth and petaloid segments - White, Corona segments Yellow or White (6) 1. J H Smith: Atholl Palace. 2. R A Scamp: S740. 3. J Goddard: Unique.

Class 159: One bloom Division 4, Perianth and petaloid segments - White, Corona segments Orange or Red. (6) 1. J Goddard: Gay Kybo. 2. R A Scamp: Gay Kybo. 3. J H Smith: Gay Kybo.

Class 160: One bloom Division 4, Perianth and petaloid segments - White, Corona segments Pink. (7) 1. B S Duncan: Dorchester. 2. Mr & Mrs D Marshall: Dorchester. 3. E Jarman: 337.

Class 161: One bloom Division 4, Perianth and petaloid segments - any colour or colours, Corona segments any colour, Cultivar not eligible for classes 156 to 160 inclusive. (0)

Class 162: One bloom, Division 5, Perianth Yellow, Corona White or Coloured. (3) 1 R A Scamp: Fairy Chimes (Best Bloom Division 5). 2. G Ridley: Fairy Chimes. 3. R Sampson: Hawera.

Class 163: One bloom, Division 5, Perianth White, Corona Coloured. (2) 1. R A Scamp: Tater Du.

Class 164: One bloom, Division 5, Perianth White, Corona White. (6) 1. Mr & Mrs D Marshall: Ice Wings. 2. Mrs J Doulton: Petrel. 3. Mrs P Cox: Petrel.

Class 165: One bloom Division 6, Perianth Yellow, Corona Yellow or White. (1) 1. M Bradbury: Elfin Gold.

Class 166: One bloom Division 6, Perianth Yellow, Corona Pink, Orange or Red. (0)

Class 167: One bloom Division 6, Perianth White, Corona Yellow. (0)

Class 168: One bloom Division 6, Perianth White, Corona Pink, Orange or Red. (7) 1. B S Duncan: Elizabeth Ann (Best Bloom Division 6). 2. R A Scamp: Betsy McDonald. 3. V & G Ellam: Elizabeth Ann.

Class 169: One bloom Division 6, Perianth White, Corona White. (0)

Class 170: One bloom Division 7, Perianth Yellow, Corona Yellow. (7) 1. R A Scamp: S729 (Best Bloom Division 7). 2. Mrs P Cox: Boscastle. 3. No award.

Class 171: One bloom Division 7, Perianth Yellow, Corona Pink, Orange or Red. (6) 1. Mrs P Cox: Mowser. 2. Mr & Mrs D Marshall: Stratosphere. 3. G Ridley: Stratosphere.

Class 172: One bloom Division 7, Perianth Yellow, Corona White, with or without a yellow rim. (6) 1. M Bird: Intrigue. 2. Mr & Mrs D Marshall: Oryx. 3. Mrs P Cox: Oryx

Class 173: One bloom Division 7, Perianth White, Corona White or Coloured. (5) 1. Mr & Mrs D Marshall: Ladies Choice. 2. Mrs P Cox: Ladies Choice. 3. M Bird: St.Pirran.

Class 174: One bloom Division 8, Perianth Yellow. (0)

Class 175: One Bloom Division 8, Perianth White. (1) 1. Mr & Mrs D Marshall: Silver Chimes (Best Bloom Division 8)

Class 176: One bloom Division 9, Perianth White. (6) 1. R A Scamp: S1035 (Best Bloom Division 9). 2. M Bird: Blisland. 3. J H Smith: Killearnan.

Class 177: One bloon Division 10 or 12, any colour combination. (0)

Class 178: One bloom Division 11, Perianth Yellow. (5) 1. Mrs P Cox: Tripartite. 2. Mrs J Doulton: Tripartite. 3. R A Scamp: Tripartite.

Class 179: One bloom Division 11, Perianth White. (1) 1. B S Duncan: 1736 (11b W-W/P) (Best Unregistered Seedling, Best Bloom Division 11).

Class 180: One bloom Cultivar with reflexing perianth, from Divisions 1 to 3. (3) 1. M Bradbury: Dawn Sky. 2. R A Scamp: S705 (2W-Y)

Class 181: One bloom Intermediate cultivar from Divisions 1 to 4. (5) 1. B S Duncan: 2099 (1Y-YYO). 2. M Bradbury: Lauren. 3. R A Scamp: S649 (3W-Y).

Class 182: One bloom Miniature Species or Wild Hybrid from Division 13. (3) 1. R A Scamp: *N. poeticus* var. *hellenicus*. 2. J W Blanchard: *N. medioluteus*. 3. M Bradbury: *N. bulbocodium*

Class 183: One bloom Miniature Cultivar (8) 1. R A Scamp: Sun Disc. 2. Mrs J Doulton: Golden Bells. 3. R Sampson: Pixies Sister.

SECTION 2 – CLASSES FOR AMATEURS

Class 184: Three Cultivars Bred and Raised by the Exhibitor, one bloom of each. (2) 1. D Turbitt: 9908 (1Y-Y), 9911 (2Y-R), 0020 (4Y-Y). 2. P Millÿ: 90/21-J (2W-WWY), 87/42-2 (2Y-W), 91/13-D (2W-YYO).

Class 185: One Cultivar Bred and Raised by the Exhibitor, one bloom. (2) 1. P Mills: 90/21-R (3W-WWY). 2. R Sampson: RPS2 (3W-YRR).

Class 186: Fifteen Cultivars, from not fewer than four Divisions, three blooms of each. (0)

Class 187: Twelve Cultivars, representing each of Divisions 1 to 4, one bloom of each. (1) 1. D Matthews: Goldfinger, Pol Voulin, Gold Convention, Dr Hugh, Sheelagh Rowan, Little Polly, Cape Point, Crowndale, Sergeants Caye,

China Doll, Jake, Savoire Faire.

Class 188: Six Cultivars, from not fewer than three Divisions, one bloom of each. (2) 1. F Verge: Dateline, S347 (1W-W), Cool Crystal, D15.1 (3Y-R), Gay Kybo, Cairntoul. 2. J Goddard: Sherpa, Gay Kybo, Dailmanach, High Society, Val d'Incles, Fragrant Rose.

Class 189: Six Cultivars, registered in or before 1980, one bloom of each. (0)

Class 190: Six Cultivars, registered in or before 1970, one bloom of each. (0)

Class 191: Six Cultivars, registered in or before 1960, one bloom of each. (0)

Class 192: Six Cultivars, registered in or before 1950, one bloom of each. (0)

Class 193: Three Cultivars, Division 1, three blooms of each. (0)

Class 194: Three Cultivars, Division 2, Yellow perianth, three blooms of each. (0)

Class 195: Three Cultivars, Division 2, White perianth, three blooms of each. (0)

Class 196: Three Cultivars, Division 3, three blooms of each. (0)

Class 197: Three Cultivars, Division 4, three blooms of each. (0)

Class 198: One Cultivar, Division 5, three blooms. (1) 1. Mrs P Cox: Mission Bells.

Class 199: One Cultivar, Division 6, three blooms. (1) 1. Mrs P Cox: Delia

Class 200: One Cultivar, Division 7, three blooms. (2) 1. J H Smith: Intrigue. 2. Mrs P Cox: Eland.

Class 201: One Cultivar, Division 8, three blooms. (0)

Class 202: One Cultivar, Division 9, three blooms. (1) 1. Mrs P Cox: Patois.

Class 203: One Cultivar, Division 10 or 12, three blooms (1) 1. Mrs J Doulton: Golden Bells (Best Bloom Division 10)

Class 204: One Cultivar, Division 11, three blooms. (0)

SECTION 3 – CLASSES FOR NOVICES

Class 205: Six Cultivars, from three or more Divisions, one bloom of each. (1) 1. D Turbitt: 0018 (2W-P), 9717 (2W-YYW), 0223 (2Y-W), 9409 (2Y-R), 9818 (2W-YP), 9411 (3W-YYO).

Class 206: Three Cultivars, Division 1, one bloom of each. (0)

Class 207: Three Cultivars, Division 2, one bloom of each. (1) 1. D Turbitt: Halstock, Ringleader, Crowndale.

Class 208: Three Cultivars, Division 3, one bloom of each. (1) 1. D Turbitt: Port Noo, Samsara, Moon Shadow.

Class 209: One bloom, Division 1, Perianth Yellow, Corona Coloured. (1) 1. D Turbitt: Inney River.

Class 210: One bloom, Division 1, Perianth Yellow, Corona White, with or without a yellow rim. (1) 1. D Turbitt: 0126

Class 211: One bloom, Division 1, Perianth White, Corona Coloured. (0)

Class 212: One bloom, Division 1, Perianth White, Corona White. (1) 1. D Turbitt: White Star.

Class 213: One bloom, Division 2, Perianth Yellow, Corona Yellow. (1) 1. D Turbitt: Coromandel.

Class 214: One bloom, Division 2, Perianth Yellow, Corona containing Pink, Orange or Red. (1) 1. D Turbitt: Ahwhanee

Class 215: One bloom, Division 2, Perianth Yellow, Corona White, with or without a yellow rim. (1) 1. D Turbitt: Altun Ha.

Class 216: One bloom, Division 2, Perianth White, Corona Yellow or White and Yellow. (1) 2. 9217

Class 217: One bloom, Division 2, Perianth White, Corona containing Pink, Orange or Red. (1) 1. D Turbitt: Mentor.

Class 218: One bloom, Division 2, Perianth White, Corona White. (1) 1. D Turbitt: Misty Glen. (Best Bloom Novice Classes)

Class 219: One bloom, Division 3, Perianth Yellow, Corona Coloured. (1) 1. D Turbitt: Badbury Rings.

Class 220: One bloom, Division 3, Perianth White, Corona Coloured. (1) 1. D Turbitt: Port Noo.

Class 221: One bloom, Division 3, Perianth White, Corona White. (0).

Class 222: One bloom, Division 4 (2) 1. D Turbitt: 0020. 2. Mrs D Scudder: unknown.

Class 223: One bloom, Division 5 (0)

Class 224: One bloom, Division 6 (1) 1. D Turbitt: 0125

Class 225: One bloom, Division 7 (1) 1. D Turbitt: Sun Disc.

Class 226: One bloom, Division 8 (0)

Class 227: One bloom, Division 9 (1) 2. D Turbitt: Campion

Class 228: One bloom, Divisions 10 or 12 (1) 1. D Turbitt: N. jonquilla.

Class 229: One bloom, Division 11 (1) 1. D Turbitt: Tripartite.

DAFFODIL SOCIETY SOUTHERN CHAMPIONSHIP THIRD LEG

Class 310: Six Cultivars, from 3 or more Divisions, one bloom of each. (1) 1. J Goddard: Sheelagh Rowan, Altun Ha, Pacific Rim, Limpopo, White Star, Coromandel.

Mitsch Daffodils

SPECIALISTS IN HYBRIDISING

YELLOW-PINKS

SPECIES HYBRIDS

AND PINK-REDS

Mr. and Mrs. Richard Havens
P.O. Box 218A
Hubbard, Oregon 97032 U.S.A.

Many cultivars from Jackson's Daffodils from Tasmania also available – acclimated to the northern hemisphere

---

Colour Catalogue published annually April – June

U.S. $4.00 (airmail) for full catalogue
Visa, Mastercard and Discover accepted

RHS Tulip Competition

Richard Smales

At the Tulip Competition on 22/23 April 2002 the number of exhibitors was disappointing. If my wife and I can bring blooms laid in a cardboard box from South Yorkshire by train, surely there are exhibitors in the south who could bring along a few flowers. They are easier to grow, dress and stage than daffodils – all you really need to do is count to six, (petals and stamens). It's very rewarding and a full bench of tulips is a joy to behold.

Only David Matthews seems to have taken up the challenge. His nine blooms of 'Olympic Flame' were placed second to Anne Smales' 'Vivex' for which she was awarded the Walter Blom Crystal Bowl. As with many other Darwinhybrids (notably the Apeldoorn family) the petals of 'Olympic Flame' do not always sit neatly on top of each other. Also one bloom was faulted because the light scarlet flashing had become very heavy. David also won the class for three pik or red tulips with 'Pink Impression'

Our 'Vivex' were far from the best we have staged, due to a basic *faux pas* when cutting. The stems were placed in a bucket with the bottoms in the corner at one end and the heads resting over the opposite rim. This is okay if only minutes are involved before the stems are carefully secured upright. For some reason a delay occurred and very quickly the stems became bowed. It seems impossible to reverse this bow. The very short (for 'Vivex') stems did not show off the blooms to the best effect. David did win the class for three pink tulips with 'Pink Impression'.

One other exhibitor is to be congratulated for making a start and we expect to see more of her in future. Jill Wright won the "three any other colour" with 'Arabian Mystery'. They were young and smallish but very fresh with good condition. The latter is a prerequisite of any floral exhibit. Nobody need be put off because their blooms are not the big, blousey specimens they probably associate with exhibition tulips. So why not pack a few tulips along with the daffodils next year and make a start?

RESULTS

Class 1 : The Walter Blom Trophy Nine blooms of one cultivar, in one vase. (3) 1. Mrs Anne Smales: Vivex. 2. D Matthews: Olympic Flame 3. Mrs Anne Smales: World's Favourite

Class 2 : Double Tulips, one cultivar, three blooms in one vase. (0) No entries

Class 3 : White Tulips, one cultivar, three blooms in one vase. (1) 1. Mrs Anne Smales: Françoise

Class 4 : Yellow Tulips, one cultivar, three blooms in one vase. (3) 1. and 2. No award 3. Mrs Anne Smales: Yellow Appeldoorn

Class 5 : Pink or Red Tulips, one cultivar, three blooms in one vase. (2) 1. D Matthews: Pink Impression 2. and 3. No award

Class 6 : Tulips of any colour, but not eligible for classes 3 to 5, one cultivar, three blooms in one vase. (1) 1. Jill Wright Arabian Mystery

Class 7 : Lily-flowered Tulips, one cultivar, three blooms in one vase. (1) Mrs Anne Smales: Ballade

Class 8 : Fringed Tulips, one cultivar, three blooms in one vase. (0) No entries

Class 9 : Viridiflora Tulips, one cultivar, three blooms in one vase. (0) No entries

Class 10 : Parrot Tulips, one cultivar, three blooms in one vase. (0) No entries

Class 11 : Kaufmanniana, Greigii or Fosteriana Tulips, one cultivar, three blooms in one vase. (0) No entries

Class 12 : Darwinhybrid Tulips, one cultivar, three blooms in one vase. (2) 1. Mrs A Smales: Queen Wilhelmena 2. No award 3. G Ridley: Not recorded

Class 13 : Any species Tulip, one pot or pan of five bulbs in bloom. (1) 1. No award 2. D Matthews: *T. clusiana* Cynthia

Other United Kingdom Shows

Daffodils and Tulips at the Harlow and Kent Shows of the Alpine Garden Society
Alan Edwards

Year on year the Narcissus season, here in the United Kingdom, seems to move forward inexorably. For example, in mid-October 2001 I had a fine pan of the Cyprus form of *N. tazetta* in full bloom and by mid-November *N. cantabricus* and its hybrids were already at their peak in the alpine house. Come the spring of 2002 this ultra-precocious trend continued at an accelerated pace following the sustained mildness of early new year.

Harlow

At the Early Spring Harlow Show on 2 March there were so many exhibits featuring members of the *jonquillae, apodanthae, ganymedes* and various tulips that it could have been a month later.

The open section always provides some glorious pans of narcissus and such was the case again this year. In the class for three pans of dwarf species or natural hybrids, a superb trio comprising *N. alpestris, N. jonquilla* var. *henriquesii* and *N. tazetta* was first with *N. asturiensis* 'Wavertree', *N. hispanicus* 'Patrick Synge' and *N. pseudonarcissus* subsp. *eugeniae* in second position. A pan virtually bursting with *N. bulbocodium*, with *N. cordubensis* MS434 and *N. bulbocodium* var. *citrinus* as runners up won the single pan class. One of my favourites, *N. moschatus* was sadly unplaced here, despite having seven stems of demurely pendant flowers. No first was awarded in the class for three pans of garden hybrids but a well deserved second went to 'Mite' 6Y-Y, 'Small Talk' 1Y-Y and Tait's venerable pre 1923 raising 'Cyclataz' 8Y-O, presumed to be the result of a union between *N. cyclamineus* and 'Soleil d'Or' 8Y-O. A generous entry of that most elegant of cyclamineus hybrids 'Mitzy' 6W-W secured first place in the single pan class with popular and dependable *N. minor* 'Douglasbank' in second and 'Pequenita' 7Y-Y in third place.

Still in the open section but with pan sizes limited to 19cm (7.5in) the class for three pans of bulbous plants of distinct genera contained several interesting items. In the winning exhibit I was attracted to *N. triandrus* var. *concolour* (possibly *N.* × *ubriquensis*), which had 30cm (12in) stems carrying two to four deep yellow flowers of typical triandrus form. The second prize entry contained an unusually tall form of *Tulipa cretica*, tinted green externally, a fine group of five white blue-eyed *Tulipa pulchella* var. *coerulea-occulata*, always a thrill to see when well grown and *N. alpestris*. Third place went to an exhibit containing *N. bulbocodium* and *Tulipa humilis violacea*. In the one pan bulbous class another green tinted *Tulipa cretica* claimed top place, with *N. canariensis* carrying umbels of three to seven sweet scented flowers in third. Unplaced but worthy of note were *Tulipa pulchella* var. *violacea* PF3503 with violet-pink, yellow eyed flowers, *T. kurdica* with almost sessile flowers of dark blood red and yet another *T. cretica* but with a reddish suffusion externally. The ubiquitous 'Elka' 1W-W, 'Gipsy Queen' 1Y-WWY and 'Midget' 1Y-Y secured first prize in the class for three pans of garden hybrids. 'Little John Walker' a possible cyclamineus hybrid with a very crenate corona, but only slightly reflexed perianth segments secured second place, supported by ample pans of 'Minicycla' 6Y-Y and 'Candlepower' 1W-W. The latter was raised by Alec Gray in 1975 and ranks among his best productions. It has relatively short-stemmed asturiensis type flowers with a pale lemon trumpet and ivory perianth segments. A huge clump of 'Jetfire' together with 'Topolino' and 'Elka' obtained third place.

There were nine entries of excellent quality in the single pan of hybrids. First prize went to a quite stunning pan of 'Minicycla' containing over 60 blooms. A good pan of the true 'Snipe' 6W-W came second. The slender grooved trumpet fades from yellow to pale lemon with age, just like 'Mitzy', whilst its narrow whitish perianth segments make a pleasing foil. In third place was 'Fairy Gold' a concolourous cyclamineus hybrid which is destined to become increasingly popular. The winning entry in the class for three pans of species or natural hybrids contained another favourite of mine, namely, *N. dubius*. The pan contained six stems, mostly with four flowers – quite an achievement! This smallest of the tazettas from the hot limestones of the South of France and North East Spain is a long job from seed but well worth the wait, believe me. Its companions were *N. jonquilla* and *N. cuatrecasasii*. In second place were good pans of *N. triandrus* subsp. *pallidulus*, *N. cazorlanus* (*N. bulbocodium* × *N. triandrus*) and *N. munozii-garmandiae*. In the one pan class the massed stems of *N. willkommii* easily triumphed, with *N. jonquilla* var. *henriquesii* in second position. In third was *N. pseudonarcissus* subsp. *eugeniae* with three stems reaching 30cm (12in), which bore little resemblance to their typically dwarfed kin in the wilds of Spain's Teruel Province. In the class for a plant rare in cultivation the much-coveted 'Trimon' 5W-W appeared sporting several well-presented greenish-yellow flowers. This apparent hybrid between *N. triandrus* and *N. cantabricus* var. *monophyllus* received an AM in 1899 (see Fig. 6)! In the next classes for material raised from seed there were commendable pans of *N. cyclamineus*, sown in January 1997, *N. alpestris* MS 542 sown in January 1994 and *N. jonquilla* var. *fernandesii*, sown in February 1995 and June 1996. *Tulipa cretica*, sown in January 1996 and *N. bulbocodium*, sown in February 1992.

The true Tenby Daffodil (*N. obvallaris*) is rarely seen at Alpine shows so it was a pleasant surprise to find it among the pans of assorted bulbs and rock plants, which obtained second prize in the six pan class. Being quite tall the species is seen to best advantage when planted informally in a woodland setting or in association with other spring flowers in a mixed border. In the class for single pans an amazingly late but sparkling white and nicely petunioid *N. cantabricus* subsp. *cantabricus* gained a first. Elsewhere in this section for those still in pursuit of a Silver Medal, first prizes were awarded to quality pans of 'Douglasbank', currently very popular with exhibitors generally, 'Snipe' and *N. papyraceus*.

Kent

A fortnight on and there were more superlative daffodil exhibits at the Kent show on 16 March. By contrast, tulips were surprisingly poorly represented this year with few on display save *T. cretica* in its slightly variant forms. Narcissus entries were dominated by jonquils and hoop petticoats, which underlined just how advanced most bulbous growth has been this spring. In the Open section a vast pan of over 100 deep yellow blooms of *N. bulbocodium* flooded the bench with golden light and gained an inevitable first. A pale form of *Tulipa cretica* with some flowers tipped with green veins came first in the class, which excluded *Fritillaria* and *Narcissus*. In the class for one pan of narcissus species or natural hybrids, *N. jonquilla* var. *henriquesii* triumphed with *N. triandrus* subsp. *triandrus* in second position and *N. bulbocodium* subsp. *conspicuus* in third. 'Mite', the slender and graceful hybrid between *N. cyclamineus* and probably the Tenby Daffodil was the winner in the class for garden hybrids with another cyclamineus hybrid, 'John Wall' second and 'Picoblanco' 2W-W third. In the class for one pan of *Tulipa* species a very pinkish *T. cretica* was second (no first awarded), third was a rather travel weary but still flamboyant *T. stapfii*. An excellent *N. cordubensis* with broad, imbricate segments, together with *N. bulbocodium* 'Mrs McConnell' secured second place in the six pan class. An exceptionally well grown pan of *N. rupicola* subsp. *watieri*, with many stems arching gracefully was first in the class for single pans of species. *N. calcicola*, also well presented was second and *N. cordubensis* third.

As at Harlow, 'Elka' was much in evidence coming first and third with 'Snipe' in second position. A few steps along the bench and there was another fine pink tinted *Tulipa cretica* in pole position. In the class for seed raised material a delightful pan of *N. alpestris* (sown 31 October 1992) earned an emphatic first. When well grown what an impact this charmer makes whenever it appears. The Ivor Barton Trophy for six pans of Monocots was won by a faultless presentation containing *N. fernandesii*, *N. nevadensis*, *N. calcicola*, and *N. dubius*; the latter with seven stems each bearing up to five flowers. A pan of *N. cyclamineus* with over 50 flowers in perfect condition was an obvious winner. Unplaced but looking really spectacular was a small group of the citron yellow *N. bulbocodium* var. *citrinus* 'Belinensis'. If very robust hoop petticoats turn you on then this is the one to grow. I have just flowered some myself for the first time this year, having obtained seed from Michael Salmon in 1997. This form comes from the Landes region in South West France and perhaps should be allocated under var. *conspicuus* according to John Blanchard. Finally, in the section reserved for members new to showing, three firsts were secured by exhibits labelled as *N. bulbocodium* var. *conspicuus*, but these all had deep yellow petticoats and in my view should be lodged under var. *obesus*.

South East England Daffodil Group Show
David Matthews

The least said about growing conditions this year the better, but although the number of exhibits was reduced, the 69 exhibitors managed to maintain a high quality of blooms.

A feature of this year's show was the sheer class of Frank Verge's flowers. Frank's superb "twelve" in the SE England Championship not only earned first place but also Best Exhibit in show. Included in this exhibit were Reserve Best Bloom in show 'Sargeant's Caye' and Best Bloom division 3 'Dateline', staged with 'Solar Tan', 'Hartlebury', 'Altun Ha', 'Gay Kybo', 'Ridgecrest', 'Celestial Fire', and 'Sharnden', and completed with two of his own seedlings and one of Michael Baxter's. Incidentally 'Sharnden's raiser Noel Burr remarked that he had never seen a better example of this fine flower.

In the Ted Osborne Memorial Class Frank's two vases of five blooms contained excellent 'Dateline', 'Evesham', 'Rockall', his own seedling, 'Altun Ha', 'Hartlebury', 'Young Blood', 'Gay Kybo', 'Hambledon' and 'Sharnden'. Frank's third major success came in the six cultivar class, where he again showed 'Sharnden', his own raising 'Mereworth', 'Young Blood', 'Altun Ha', 'Moon Shadow' and 'Dateline'. Halting Frank's clean sweep of the major trophies I thwarted his chances in the class for three vases of three blooms using 'Gold Convention', 'Val d'Incles' and 'Goldfinger'; Frank's 'Cool Crystal', 'Young Blood' and 'Altun Ha' were a close second. Frank breaks all the conventional rules: - he plants very early, never waters, cuts blooms in bud, and transports them massed in buckets! Is this where the rest of us all go wrong?

It was good to see John Goddard back on form, winning the class for six doubles with 'Gay Kybo', two 'Unique', an unknown cultivar, 'Marjorie Treveal' and 'Dorchester'. John also won the class for two vases of three blooms from divisions 5-9 with eye-catching 'Ice Wings' in both vases, staged with 'Stratosphere', 'Kaydee' and 'Swallow Wing'.

Mid Southern's impressive exhibit was the winning entry in the SE England Inter-Society Championship, maintaining their unbroken run of wins, although they were strongly challenged by Haywards Heath HS. Malcolm

Bradbury was successful in the class for three blooms raised outside Europe beating ten other good entries with 'Bandit', 'Trumpet Warrior' and 'Conestoga'

The class for three cultivars from the same raiser was won by Steve Holden whose colourful exhibit of 'China Doll', 'Chelsea Girl' and 'Royal China' were all raised by Clive Postles

'Silent Valley' earned first place for Barry Ridsdale in the class for three white daffodils ahead of a strong field. 'Silent Valley' also featured in Barry's winning entry in the class calling for one bloom from each of divisions. 1-4 in the Smaller Growers' section, where 'High Society', 'Purbeck' and 'Gay Kybo' completed the quartet. Barry continued his success by gaining most points in the eight multi-bloom classes. The seedling section was again strongly contested, and included the Best Bloom in show and Best Unregistered Seedling, an outstanding 2Y-R raised and shown by John Gibson in his winning collection of six seedlings. Noel Burr's well-balanced trio received the honours in the three seedlings class, whilst Steve Holden's 3Y-Y justifiably won the single seedling class.

Miniature Championship

Having increased the number of classes for Miniatures to include a Miniature Championship, it was heartening to see 15 exhibitors competing. Janine Doulton scored most points in the six classes, and also deservedly won the Championship class for three vases of three blooms with 'Xit', 'Fairy Chimes' and 'Rikki'.

Single Bloom classes

The single bloom classes were well filled and included many excellent flowers. Of particular note were John Parkinson's 'Goldfinger' and 'Pacific Rim', Malcolm Bradbury's 'Uncle Duncan', Steve Holden's 'Elmbridge', 'Castle Howard' and 'Crowndale', David Vivash's 'Sergeants Caye', Pam Cox's 'Ringleader', Phil Baxter's 'Nonchalant', and Noel Burr's P3-50-90 3W-Y and 'Hever', Ron Allen's 'Soprano'

won a large class in which it was good to see such a wide variety of cultivars. Steve Holden's showed a lovely 'Cherrygardens' as a non-predominant pink, and his beautifully formed 'Gay Kybo' was Best Bloom in division 4. Notable flowers in the species based divisions were Malcolm Bradbury's well refrigerated 'Rapture' and Geoff Ridley's 'Sheer Joy' and 'Stratosphere'. Pam Cox is to be congratulated on receiving most points in the Single Bloom classes - not an easy achievement.

Smaller Growers Section

From the 109 entries in the Smaller Growers Section a tie for points resulted between Fred White and George Kimber. Julia and Steve Holden who donate the award for this each year, very kindly purchased a second piece of crystal, enabling both exhibitors to have a memento of their success. Brian Everest's 'Gay Kybo' received the award for Best Bloom in the section, whilst Fred White won the six showing very good 'Cool Crystal', 'Fire-Blade', 'Ring Fence', 'June Lake', 'Soprano' and 'Goldfinger'.

Novices

On to the Novices where Best Bloom in the Section and also deservedly Best Bloom divisions 5-11 were awarded to Ray Sedgwick's pristine 'Ice Wings'. Tod Frost had the most novice points, winning four of the six classes with good quality blooms. The classes were supported by 16 exhibitors who had travelled from all over the South East.

THE DAFFODIL SOCIETY ANNUAL SHOW
JAN DALTON

It was not without a tinge of trepidation that the Society embarked on its journey to our new venue at Myton School, Warwick on the weekend of 20-21 April. This was to be the first show for almost 30 years that the Society would be staging on its own since forming the long and fruitful relationship with Solihull

Horticultural Society in the early 1970s. Unfortunately the need to expand our own show area and the fact that no other suitable venue had been identified in the Solihull area that would accommodate both shows comfortably, meant a parting of the ways. Equally we had suffered a major setback at the hands of "big business", when our original supposed new venue at a prime location garden centre had fallen through due to a takeover of the Garden Centre chain by a larger conglomerate – caveat emptor!

Little wonder then, when our Show Manager and his team arrived at the school on the Friday afternoon, to set up the staging, that the pulse began to race and the heartbeat increased at the sight of a fire-engine and several police cars attending the school grounds. However all fears were happily allayed when it turned out that the school had not in fact burnt down and that the presence of the emergency services was nothing more than an educational visit. Once this initial scare had been forgotten, the show was well and truly on and our new staging, hand-made by John Gibson our Show Manager, again proved its worth by being erected in a very short space of time.

Trade Stand
In an era where specialist daffodil suppliers seem to be decreasing in number and daffodil trade stands in general are getting fewer every season, it was a delight to see such a magnificent display as that staged by Ron and Maureen Scamp of Falmouth. In prime position in the centre of the main hall, Ron and Maureen exhibited 72 vases of Cornish grown daffodils, many of Ron's own raising, with no repetition of cultivars. The colour and divisional range was a sight to behold and their efforts were rewarded by a unanimous decision to award them The Daffodil Society Gold Medal.

Competitive Classes – Major Trophies
The Bourne Cup for twelve cultivars raised by the exhibitor, had three good entries with Clive Postles making a welcome return to the show benches to take the honours. Two of Clive's best flowers were doubles and one of these, 1-5-89 4Y-YYO, was eventually selected as the Best Unregistered seedling in show, thus receiving the F E Board Trophy; Peter Mills was second and Ron Scamp third. Ron included some interesting flowers from divisions 7 and 9, one of which S725 received the rosette for Best Poeticus hybrid.

In another very early season that saw many exhibitors from the South without flowers, it was not surprising to see no entries in the Society's Centenary Class for nine vases of three blooms and similarly in the Amateur section for the de Navarro Cup for six vases of three blooms. Richard Smales was the most successful exhibitor in the remaining multi-bloom classes, winning the F E Board Memorial Award for three vases of three blooms from three divisions and also most points in the Crystal Trophy classes for individual vases of three blooms from divisions 1-4. Richard also had Best Bloom division 3 with an 'Achduart' 3Y-R from his unplaced exhibit in these classes.

The most successful exhibitor overall in the Open collection classes was Roger Braithwaite who took the Cartwright Cup for twelve cultivars in commerce, The Leamington Cup for six cultivars with red or orange coronas, The Walter Ware Vase for six pinks and the White Daffodil Trophy for six white trumpets. Roger's 'White Star' in the latter was Best Bloom in division 1.

Miniatures
Not to be outdone by her partner, Terry Braithwaite took the Miniature Challenge Trophy for three vases of three species and/or cultivars and also the rosette for Best Miniature in show with 'Hawera' 5Y-Y.

Harry Fogg had an amazing win with his vase of three 'Fairy Chimes' 5Y-Y which received the diploma for the Best Vase of Miniatures, the Society's Silver Medal for the Best Vase of one cultivar in show and the Bikini Trophy for the Best Vase in show! Quite an achievement.

Single Blooms

These were the usual mix of high and low entries according to division, which reflected the early season. Trumpets were in short supply and good trumpets even scarcer, the best of these being a nice 'Trumpet Warrior' 1YYW-WWY. Division 2 on the other hand, brought some much better flowers including the Premier Bloom in show, Colin Gilman's 'Sheelagh Rowan' 2W-W. This magnificent bloom was easily the winner in its class and outshone all the other divisional rosette winners to take the top honour the Jim Pearce Award for Best Bloom in show as well as the Woodward Cup for Best Bloom shown by an amateur.

Dennis and Gill Marshall won the Sarah Dear Trophy for the Best Pink-Cupped division 2 with 'Cape Point' and the rosette for Best Bloom division 5 with 'Ice Wings' 5W-W. Reg Chantry's 'Stratosphere' 7Y-O and Steve Holden's 'Tripartite' were also worthy winners of divisional Best Bloom awards and I was particularly pleased to see my own twin-headed *N. ernii* (*N. triandrus* subsp. *triandrus* × *N. bulbocodium* subsp. *bulbocodium*) take the rosette for Best Bloom division 13.

The Ralph White Memorial Award for most points in the single bloom classes went to Dennis and Gill Marshall and the runner-up, for the Bronze Medal was Ted Perran who also had Best Bloom division 8 with 'Silver Chimes' and won the American Daffodil Society Ribbon in the overseas classes.

Amateur, Restricted and Novice Classes

In the Amateur and restricted classes Keith Capper took the Wooton Cup for twelve cultivars, one stem of each, beating some strong opposition. Keith also won the Post and Mail Trophy for three whites from any division, and also staged the winning exhibit on behalf of the North Manchester Bar Top Group to gain the Peter Lower Cup for twelve cultivars from an affiliated society.

Mick Henson won the Norfolk Cup for twelve cultivars chosen from our new list of *Approved Cultivars for Restricted Classes* (this replaced the previous Price Limit list) and it was pleasing to see that all the entries staged in this class complied with the list. Mick also won the GKN Challenge Bowl for the all-yellow cultivars.

The most successful Novice grower was newcomer Keith Boxall who took the Bronze Medal for Most Points in the section. Keith was also the first recipient of the Dan du Plessis Memorial Trophy, newly presented by Dan's two daughters Marie and Paula and the du Plessis family. Dan was a great supporter of the Society and the show and always encouraged new growers to exhibit and I am sure that he would have approved.

There were many other prizewinners, too numerous to mention, but suffice to say all contribution to an excellent show and more than pleased with the new venture.

New Technology

The Society not only moved forward by way of a change of venue and location but it very much entered the realms of the computer age this year. All entries, cup cards, trophy winners and points administration etc was very ably conducted by James Akers and his computer hardware or should it be software? There can be little doubt that the exercise was a great success for a first attempt and providing the operator is computer literate there seems to be no limit to what the technology can do for labour-saving administration.

So ended another show, with all our staging tucked away in its own on-site cubby-hole, where it will remain ready for next years show. All we need to do now, is attract the public to our future shows by way of advance publicity and other knowledge that the Myton School will hopefully become our permanent venue for many years to come.

Daffodils and Tulips at Harrogate Spring Show
Wendy Akers

For most exhibitors the ups and downs of daffodil flowering each year have always culminated in the Harrogate Show. This year's show on 25-28 April confirmed the trend of warmer weather and earlier flowering. When I first started showing at Harrogate some 20 years ago I could never get small cups and doubles open and in desperation often showed division 3s that I had forced open from pencil buds. Nowadays, we seem to be praying over the daffodil beds that there will be any left to show by the end of April.

Collection classes

More kudos then to Roger Braithwaite for his North of England Championship triumph. There were six entries and I think Roger's was the best he's put up for some time, they had the weight and were so well balanced. He had two Best Blooms, 'Moon Shadow' which became Grand Champion Bloom in show as well as Best Bloom division 3 and 'Goldfinger', Best Bloom division 1. He also included the best 'Purbeck' I've seen for ages, a super 'Jake', an exquisite 'Royal China' and a lovely 'Best Friend'. Reg Chantry, 2.5 points behind Roger had the iciest white 'Cool Crystal', another very round 'Moon Shadow' and the elegant 'Sheelagh Rowan'.

The six entries in the all-whites were a lovely sight; all the winning sixes included Fred Board's lovely 'Misty Glen'. Jeff Stuart's growing skills gained him first prize.

In the class for six from the higher divisions, Mr McDonald, who was third, was up against two top showing ladies, Mrs Parsons and Terry Braithwaite. Mrs Parson's winning set had all multi-headed triandrus and jonquil hybrids, which looked charming and included a beautiful 'Petrel'. Terry had a superb 'Eland' and a gorgeous 'Lilac Charm'.

The Derbyshire area where Roger comes from must have hit the season right because Ilkeston won the society class with a superb twelve, which were a whole 16 points ahead of the competition.

Single blooms

Looking through the single bloom classes a significant number of lovely seedlings were evident throughout. The 3Y-Y class was won by a really smooth 'Ferndown' of Rae Beckwith but closely followed by Alec Harper's seedling 92-2-20D with a mid-yellow even cup. Again, in the class for 3Y-R the winner was Ken Bowser's majestic 'Samsara', second was a seedling D1661 shown by Mrs Val Stuart. The third place was taken by arguably the best 'Achduart' I've ever seen shown by Reg Chantry and it was interesting to compare the perianths, the seedling had a slightly more intense yellow cup. A couple of seedlings slugged it out in the class for division 3 white perianths with a rim. Triumphant was Len Tomlinson's VR939, it had a huge perianth and pale yellow cup with a defined rim, all in excellent balance. Alec Harper's seedling No 11 had an icy white perianth and a white cup with a glowing rim of pinky orange. Now, when did a triandrus last win Reserve Grand Champion? Again, a seedling of Alec Harper's, 96-2-23C (*N. triandrus* var. *triandrus* × 'Limequilla') a beautiful flower with all the grace of the triandrus species in a uniform primrose yellow took that honour. Alec must be feeling satisfied that his years of hybridizing are bearing such impressive fruit.

In the Jim Akers' class for unregistered seedlings Ken Bowser had a 'Rainbow' × 'Dailmanach' cross which had good pose and an exquisite creamy pink cup and Jeff Stuart had an interesting 'Colley Gate' × 'Verona' seedling which I described in my notes as "white, green, yellow, red rim, like a poeticus writ large". I must mention finally my favourite of Alec's delightful seedlings, many of which have one species parent. This won the class for a cultivar raised by the exhibitor from divisions 5, 7 or 8 and was a triandrus 97-2-11B (*N. triandrus* var. *triandrus* × 'Quick Step') with five graceful pendent heads. Really, we are used to seeing good seedlings at the London shows but it was great pleasure to see so many from all the divisions at Harrogate.

Tulips

After a slight blip last year caused by the late season, the sixth tulip show maintained its ever increasing popularity with 30 exhibitors entering a total of 149 vases or pots. The Tulip Championship of Great Britain for three cultivars, nine blooms of each, was being held for the fourth year and so far no competitor has been successful for a second time. There were eleven exhibits this year and no one was more surprised than me to be placed first with vases of 'Vivex', 'World's Favourite' and 'Mirella'. In second place was Liz Tomlinson showing 'World's Favourite', 'Big Smile' and 'Pink Impression'; Chris Bone was third with 'Golden Apeldoorn', 'Françoise' and 'Long Lady'. 'World's Favourite', the winning cultivar for James Akers in the single vase of nine tulips, is beginning to rival its fellow Darwinhybrid 'Vivex' as the top show cultivar but the competition in this class was also very strong with 16 entries. Mrs Pat King was second with the Single Late 'Caravelle' and Teresa Clements third with the yellow Triumph 'Golden Melody'. This was Teresa's first ever tulip show and she also gained third prize in the two classes which attracted the highest number of entries, those for three lily flowered which had 18 and the class for three pink or red, where there were 24. The lily flowered class was won by local exhibitor Caroline Wright's 'Pieter de Leur' and the red/pink by Anne Smales' 'Vivex'; overall quite a "Ladies Day" for the tulip exhibitors.

BELFAST SPRING FLOWER SHOW
JAMES SMYTH

The Belfast Show on 20-21 April was held in Malone House in Barrett's Demesne. Here we welcomed Rae Beckwith and Dale Griffen as guest judges to our show. With Brian Duncan and Nial Watson at the World Convention in America, the field was open for some serious competition. Despite the strong winds and heavy rain in the second half of the week, we had a great show with quality and quantity too, with approximately 1,150 blooms being shown.

Open Classes

The Open Championship of Ireland had eight entries and was won by Richard McCaw. His twelve flowers were seedling 12 3Y-Y (Best Bloom division 3 and Best Seedling in show), 'Amazing Grace', 'Auspicious', 'Dorchester', 'Nether Barr', 'Crowndale', 'Purbeck', 'Goldfinger, 'Ahwahnee', 'June Lake', 'Dateline' and 'Ridgecrest'. John O'Reilly was second and included good specimens of 'Altun Ha', 'Barbary Gold' and 'Filoli'. Sandy McCabe was third and included two flowers which won best bloom awards. 'Ethos' 1Y-Y (Best Bloom division 1) and 'Dorchester (Best Bloom division 4).

The Royal Mail Trophy, for six vases of three blooms of Irish-raised cultivars, was hotly contested. Sandy McCabe was the winner with 'Ringleader', 'Dunadry Inn' and 'Goldfinger' the best flowers in his line up. Richard McCaw was second including 'Barnesgold', 'Angelito' and a good 2W-OOR seedling of his own raising. Robbie Curry was third with good 'Chobe River' and 'Serena Beach'.

Richard McCaw won the class for five American-raised cultivars with 'River Queen', 'Berceuse', 'Verran Rose', 'Limpkin' and 'Presidential Pink'. Ian Scroggy was placed second and Kate Reade third.

The Guy Wilson Trophy for three vases of three blooms of all-white cultivars was won by

Derrick Turbitt with 'White Star', 'Misty Glen' and 'Silver Crystal'. Second was Maurice Kerr with 'Burntollet', 'White Tea' and 'Silver Surf' and third was James Smyth with 'Silver Crystal', 'Regal Bliss' and 'Portfolio'.

There were ten entries for the Gilbert Andrew's Award which calls for six cultivars, one stem of each. Robbie Currie's winning entry was 'Altun Ha', 'Young Blood', 'Dr Hugh', 'Badbury Rings', seedling 5-30-2 and 'Cool Crystal' 3W-W.

The International Award, presented by the S E England Daffodil Group for three vases of three blooms raised outside Ireland was won by John O'Reilly with 'Altun Ha', 'Holme Fen' and 'Filoli'.

This year the schedule was changed to combine the Open and Amateur three bloom classes and as a result attracted 127 entries across the 18 classes. The Best Vase of Three Blooms was 'Barnesgold' 1Y-Y exhibited by Richard McCaw. Other good vases included Robbie Curry's 'White Star', Maurice Kerr's 'Purbeck' and 'Tuesday's Child', Sandy McCabe's 'Colourful' and 'Dunkery', James Smyth's 'Badbury Rings' and George Wilson's 'Savoir Faire'.

Single Bloom Classes
The single blooms from amateur and open sections were also combined attracting 333 blooms, including Best Bloom in show and Best division 2, 'Fragrant Rose' 2W-GPP exhibited by Ian Erskine from Dublin. Other good blooms from this section were John O'Reilly's 'Goldfinger', and 'Dorchester'; Maurice Kerr's 'Kingsgrove', 'Ardress' and a seedling 2W-GYR; Sandy McCabe's 'Burntollet', 'Gold Bond' and 'Chinchilla'; Michael Ward's 'Korora Bay' and 'Fireblade'; Derrick Turbitt's 2Y-R seedling and 'Dunley Hall'; James Smyth's 'Nonchalant', 'Crowndale' and 'Tuesday's Child'; George Wilson's 'Achduart' and 'Ravenhill'; Robbie Curry's 3Y-YYR seedling and 'Serena Beach' and lastly but by no means least Richard McCaw's 'Lilac Charm' 6W-GPP which was Best Bloom from divisions 5-11.

Amateur Collection Classes
The Amateur Championship of Ireland was very hotly contested with eight strong entries causing a real headache for the judging panel. Eventually Maurice Kerr won the title with seven of his own seedlings. This shows that Maurice's breeding programme is producing flowers capable of holding their own against established cultivars. Richard McCaw was second with good examples of 'Ahwahnee', 'Serena Beach' and 'Barnesgold'. Robbie Curry was third with 'Ethos' and 'Evesham' in his line-up.

In the class for six vases of three blooms Richard McCaw took the honours with good vases of 'Evesham', 'Ahwahnee' and 'Ita'. Sandy McCabe was second with 'Altun Ha' and an 'Ethos' × 'Goldfinger' 1Y-Y seedling his best flowers. James Smyth was third with an entry which included a very colourful vase of 'Topkapi'.

The amateur class for American-raised cultivars was won by George Wilson with 'Daydream', 'Silken Sails', 'Beautiful Dream', 'Intrigue' and 'Hoopoe'.

Novice Classes
Two competitors dominated this section. Ted Thompson won the Novice Championship of Ireland and the award for Most Points in the section. Tracy Hamilton from Killyleagh won the Best Vase of Three Blooms award with 'Badbury Rings' 3Y-YYR and also the Best Bloom in the Novice section with 'Port Noo' 3W-Y.

Silver Thread Award
Fermanagh Garden Society show hosted the award this year and as a result attracted many more exhibitors than usual with almost 500 blooms being shown and with 16 winning exhibitors. The class calls for three vases of three blooms and was won by John Ennis with 'Purbeck', 'Mount Fuji' and 'Goldfinger'. In second place was Richard McCaw and third was Robbie Curry.

The Wakefield and North of England Tulip Society 167th Annual Show
James Akers

Until about ten years ago, the local members decided the date of this show so that account was taken of the current season. In Victorian times they met weekly in April and May until a consensus was reached and the show day agreed: as a result it is possible from looking back at these dates to get some idea of the pattern of the seasons going back over 150 years. Although the average show-date is just after the middle of May, there is a wide variation with three shows being held in the second week of June and in 1879 it was held on 16 June. Only once since 1917, on 2 June 1941, has the show been held in that month and the earliest recorded shows were held on 5 May 1945 and 8 May 1943. Because so few members now live in the Wakefield area the show date of 18 May was decided upon in October. However as a result of global warming or whatever, the show should ideally have been held at the end of April. By means of refrigeration, a record number of 37 exhibitors from around the country still managed to preserve flowers to place on the show bench.

Vase classes

In this section, which is mainly for tulips other than English Florists', there were a total of 45 entries. This was slightly fewer than last year, and consisted almost entirely of late flowering cultivars. The winner of the John Hardman Memorial Vase for a vase of 18 tulips was, for the second successive year, Mrs Pat King with 'Menton'. In second place was Andrew McDougal with 'Maureen' and third Anne Turner with an unknown cultivar. In the class for twelve tulips 'Menton' and 'Maureen' were again placed first and second with both entries being by Barbara Pickering. The 'Menton' were awarded the Peter Emmett Trophy for Best Vase in this section. Pat King's third place together with her winning entries in both the six and three bloom classes gave her the award for Most Points in the section.

Florists Tulips

Growing a bed of over a thousand seedling breeders on a north facing slope enabled John Wainwright to dominate the classes for un-broken tulips. John was the first prize winner in the twelve, six and three breeder classes, with seedlings, which was sufficient to ensure that he gained enough points to win the Jim Akers Memorial goblet for Most Points in the Open section. The single breeder class was won by Beryl Royles showing one of husband Peter's seedlings, 98 which was awarded Best Breeder in show.

The class for twelve rectified tulips, two feathers and two flames from each of the three colour types, rose, bybloemen and bizarre had only one entry my own, but was adjudged worthy of first place. The best flower in this entry was a 'Wakefield' flamed which became Best Flame and overall Best Bloom in show. There were three entries in the class for nine blooms, breeder flame and feather from each of the colour types with Sarah Wainwright placed first, Judy Baker second and John Snocken third. I was successful in the class for six rectified and included a 'Royal Sovereign' that was made Best Feather in show. This cultivar is one of the last to flower on the bed, was raised around 1810, and a painting of it appears in the *Floricultural Cabinet*. Jane Green's winning flamed 'Talisman' won the Cochrane of Cults Vase for the Best Bloom in the single bloom classes and was in contention with the 'Wakefield' for Best Flame, losing out probably only because it was not fully open. Few good 'Talisman' flowers have been seen over the past 30 years, so it is hoped that Jane will manage to get good increase from this rectified clone.

Good rectified flowers are in short supply so it was encouraging to see Sarah Wainwright exhibit for the first time in her winning nine, a

103

new bybloemen of my raising, 'Rory McEwen' flamed (see Fig. 12). Sarah has built up a moderate stock of this cultivar that hopefully will be distributed among the Society members over the next few years. Also encouraging were two newly broken feathered seedlings, shown by husband John, which were awarded second place in the class for a pair of feathers and also a feathered seedling 30, from Beryl Royles which was also placed second in the single feather class.

After over ten years of trying, Kate Swift gained sufficient points in the Novice section to win the Glass Goblet and also repeated that success in the Extra-Open section. 'James Wild' was the cultivar that won the Best Bloom awards in both these sections, a feather for David Tarver in the Novices and a flame for Emily Baker, the youngest exhibitor, in the Extra-Open section.

Anna Pavord opened the show and congratulated the Society on once more producing an excellent display of this unique flower, the English Florists' tulip. She was confident that the future of the Society was assured because of the new flowers she had seen on the showbench and the young exhibitors who were among the prize winners.

TULIP DAY

The Royal Horticultural Society will hold a Tulip Day on

Wednesday 30th April 2003

RHS Lawrence Hall, Greycoat Street, Westminster, London SW1

Anna Pavord on the History of the Tulip

Brian Mathew on Species Tulips

Chris Blom on Modern Tulips, Growing in the Garden and Producing a Display at Chelsea (see Fig. 27)

James Akers on Florist Tulips and on Showing Tulips

Tulip displays

Demonstrations

Cost £15, including free admission to the RHS London Flower Show on the same day
For further information contact:
Georgina Clarke, RHS Shows Department Tel: 020 7821 3328
Also see the 'Gardens and Events' section of the RHS Journal, *The Garden*.

Awards

Wisley Daffodil Trials
David Matthews

The daffodil trials this year were notable for the health of the plants throughout the trials period, thanks to the field staff and to the sterilized soil in which they were planted, culminating in a truly wonderful display of flowers.

At its meeting on 5 June 2002, the Daffodil and Tulips Trials Sub-Committee recommended that the Award of Garden Merit (AGM) as a flowering plant for garden decoration be given to the eight cultivars listed below. The recommendation was subsequently ratified by Council. Abbreviated comments from members of the Trials Sub-Committee are given in italics after the details of each cultivar.

Award of Garden Merit

N. 'Silent Valley' 1W-GWW raised by Tom Bloomer, sent for trial by J S Pennings, Schorweg 14, 1764 MC De Bilt Breezand, The Netherlands. *"Flowering from 2 April to 26 April, this is a strong plant with a very good impact for both garden use and exhibition".*

N. 'Unique' 4W-Y sent by R A Scamp, Quality Daffodils, 14 Roscarrack Close, Falmouth, Cornwall. *"Flowering from 12 April to 14 May, this is an early flowering double that holds its head up well on a strong stem, and keeps the colour strongly throughout the season".*

N. 'Drumlin' 1W-Y raised and sent by Ballydorn Bulb Farm, Killinchy, Newtownards, Co. Down, Northern Ireland. *"Flowering from 12 April to 14 May this flower has great impact, being a tall and strong plant with a long flowering period".*

N. 'Manly' 4Y-O raised by the late J L Richardson and sent by Bloms Bulbs, Primrose Nurseries, Melchbourne, Bedford. *"This is a flower of impressive size with great impact for the garden, the flowers are held well on strong stems; flowering from 14 April to 14 May".*

N. 'Boslowick' 11aY-O raised and sent by R A Scamp. *"This flower is a split corona of great presence, excellent for garden and exhibition use, flowering from 1 April to 4 May".*

N. 'Lemon Drops' 5Y-Y raised by G E Mitsch USA and sent by Bloms Bulbs. *"The flowers open pale yellow but fade to white; ideal for the garden the plants being very floriferous with blooms lasting a long time, flowering from 12 April to 14 May".*

N. 'Dickcissel' 7Y-W raised by G E Mitsch USA and sent by Bloms Bulbs. *"Flowering from 8 April to 14 May this multi-headed cultivar is very free flowering, with the blooms held well above the foliage, and is good for exhibition, floral art, cut flower and garden use".*

N. 'Hoopoe' 8Y-O raised by G E Mitsch and sent by R Nicholl, 17 Orchard Avenue, Rainham, Essex. *"This variety is widely available, and has two or three florets per stem. It is a very durable flower with lots of impact, flowering from 6 April to 4 May".*

Three other cultivars - 'Pipit', 'High Society' and 'Precocious' again received marks meriting an AGM, but had already received the award in 2001 following a recommendation from the Daffodil and Tulip Committee.

Everyone on the Daffodil and Tulip Trials Sub Committee would like to wish Anne Smith the Trials Recorder, a long and happy retirement. Her willingness and enthusiasm for her job far exceeded all normal expectations and we shall all miss her.

Awards Given by RHS Committees

Award of Merit
Narcissus
Daffodil and Tulip Committee, as a hardy flowering plant for exhibition.
N. **'Camoro' 10WWG-W AM** 18 December 2001. Exhibited by The Rock Garden Department, RHS Garden, Wisley, Woking.
N. **'Littlefield' 7O-GOO AM** 23 April 2002. Exhibited by R.A.Scamp (see Fig. 10).

Galanthus
Joint Rock Garden Plant Committee, as a hardy flowering plant for exhibition.
G. **'Cowhouse Green' AM** 19 February 2002. Exhibited by Dr R Mackenzie, Barn Cottage, Shilton, Oxfordshire.

Preliminary Commendation
Joint Rock Garden Plant Committee, as a hardy flowering plant for exhibition.
Narcissus **'Eira' 12W-W, PC** 18 September 2001. Exhibited 10 March 2001 by Dr & Mrs R.B.Wallis, Llwyn Ifan, Porthyrhyd, Carmarthen, Dyfed SA32 8BP

Members of the RHS Daffodil and Tulip Committee after their meeting on 23 April.
Back row (left to right): Peter Brandham, Ron Scamp, Nial Watson, Jan Pennings, Malcolm Bradbury, Jan Dalton, Eddie Jarman, David Matthews, Noel Burr and Sally Kington (Committee Secretary and International Daffodil Registrar)
Seated (left to right): Ron Blom, Reg Nicholl, Christine Skelmersdale, Brian Duncan (Chairman), John Blanchard (Vice-Chairman) and Jim Pearce
Members unable to be present on this occasion were John Pearson (Vice-Chairman), James Akers, Gordon Hanks, George Tarry and Johnny Walkers

DAFFODIL & TULIP COMMITTEE 2002

CHAIRMAN

Duncan, B S, Knowehead, 15 Ballynahatty Road, Omagh, Co Tyrone, N Ireland BT78 1PN

VICE-CHAIRMEN

Blanchard, J W, Old Rectory Garden, Shillingstone, Blandford, Dorset DT11 0SL
Pearson, A J R, Hofflands, Little Totham Rd, Goldhanger, Maldon, Essex CM9 8AP

MEMBERS

Akers, J L, 70 Wrenthorpe Lane, Wrenthorpe, Wakefield, West Yorkshire WF2 0PT
Blom, R J M, Birwell Lodge, Shelton, Huntingdonshire PE18 0NR
Bradbury, M S, The Well House, 38 Powers Hall End, Witham, Essex CM8 1LS
Brandham, Dr P, Jodrell Laboratory, Royal Botanic Gardens, Kew, Richmond, Surrey TW9 3DS
Burr, N A, Rushers Cottage, Rushers Cross, Mayfield, East Sussex TN20 6PX
Dalton, J, 34 Conan Drive, Richmond, North Yorkshire DL10 4PQ
Hanks, G, HRI, Willington Road, Kirton, Lincolnshire PE20 1NN
Jarman, E, Clover Meadows, Treraven Lane, Wadebridge, Cornwall PL27 7JZ
Matthews, D, 35 Hazeldown Close, River, Dover, Kent CT17 0NJ
Nicholl, R, 17 Orchard Avenue, Rainham, Essex RM13 9NY
Pearce, D J, 1 Dorset Cottages, Birch Road, Copford, Colchester, Essex CO6 1DR
Pennings, J S, Schorweg 14, 1764 MC De Bilt, Breezand, The Netherlands
Scamp, R, 14 Roscarrack Close, Falmouth, Cornwall TR11 4PJ
Skelmersdale, Lady, Barr House, Bishops Hull, Taunton, Somerset TA4 1AE
Tarry, G W, Cresta, Well Lane, Ness, Neston CH64 4AW
Walkers, J, Broadgate, Weston Hills, Spalding, Lincs PE12 6DQ
Watson, N A C, Ringhaddy Lodge, Killinchy, Co Down, N Ireland BT23 6TU
Secretary Kington, Mrs S, RHS, 80 Vincent Square, London SW1P 2PE

NARCISSUS CLASSIFICATION ADVISORY COMMITTEE 2002

Chairman Duncan, B S
Vice Chairman Blanchard, J W
Bradbury, M S
Brickell, C D
Dalton, J
Gripshover, Mrs M L

Lemmers, W
Nicholl, R
Pearce, D J
Secretary Kington, Mrs S
Ex officio Leslie, A C

INDEX

Authors	Page
Akers, James	
DAFFODILS, SNOWDROPS AND TULIPS	7
CANADIAN TULIP FESTIVAL	29
BOOK REVIEWS – ADS Illustrated Databank	70
WNOE Tulip Society 167th Annual Show	103
Akers, Wendy	
Daffodils and Tulips at Harrogate Spring Show	100
Bankhead, Delia	
Are These Miniature Daffodils Extinct?	71
Baker, Ruby	
A New Yellow Snowdrop	72
Bishop, Matt	
STARTING A SNOWDROP COLLECTION	57
Blanchard, John	
SPANISH RHAPSODY	14
Display of Miniature Species and Hybrid *Narcissi*	78
Bradbury, Malcolm	
DIVISION 9 - A SYMPOSIUM – Overview	20
BOOK REVIEWS	
New Zealand Daffodil Annual 2002	70
ADS Honours Sally Kington	71
Brandham, Peter	
TRIPLOIDY IN *NARCISSUS*	50
Narcissus dubius as Breeding Material	73
Chappell, Daphne	
The Cottage Garden Society Snowdrop Group	72
Dalton, Jan	
WORDSWORTH'S DAFFODILS	13
THE SEARCH FOR *N. LAGOI*	18
The Daffodil Society Annual Show	97
Davis, Tony	
AUSTRALIA SPEAKING WITH ONE VOICE	54
de Jager, R. Degenaar	
THE HORTUS BULBORUM SHOWS THE GRAND HISTORY OF BULBS	8
Duncan, Brian	
THE PETER BARR MEMORIAL CUP 2002	65
Edwards, Alan	
Daffodils and Tulips at AGS Shows	94
Galyon, Frank B	
MY WORK WITH THE GENUS *NARCISSUS*	45
Goddard, John	
RHS Early Daffodil Competition	81
Gripshover, Mary Lou	
DIVISION 9 - A SYMPOSIUM	
Poeticus Hybrids in the USA	25
Hamilton, Max	
DIVISION 9 - A SYMPOSIUM	
New Zealand Poets	26
Hanks, Gordon	
GROWING HEALTHIER DAFFODILS	43
Kington, Sally	
VINTAGE DOUBLES	37
Lebsa, Jörg	
YET ANOTHER *GALANTHUS ELWESII*?	61
Leeds, Rod	
BOOK REVIEWS	
Snowdrops: A Monograph of Cultivated *Galanthus*	67
Leslie, Alan	
Snowdrops at the RHS February Show	79
Matthews, David	
South East England Daffodil Group Show	96
AWARDS – Wisley Daffodil Trials	105
McGregor, Jim	
A YEAR IN THE LIFE OF *NARCISSUS RUPICOLA* SUBSP. *WATIERI*	11
Nicholl, Reg	
RHS Daffodil Show	85
Page, John	
THE NOMENCLATURE OF SPECIES TULIPS	33
Pennings, Jan	
THE FLORIADE	55
Perrignon, Richard	
DIVISION 9 - A SYMPOSIUM	
Division 9 in Australia	27
Ramsay, Peter	
The Daffodil Society Cultural Guide	68
Scamp, Ron	
DIVISION 9 - A SYMPOSIUM	
Poeticus Ramblings	23
OBITUARY – John Daniel du Plessis	66
Skelmersdale, Christine	
DIVISION 9 - A SYMPOSIUM	
Narcissus poeticus in the garden	27
Smales, Richard	
BOOK REVIEWS – Tulip	67
BOOK REVIEWS – Tulips	67
RHS Tulip Competition	93
Smyth, James	
Belfast Spring Flower Show	101
Watson, Nial	
DIVISION 9 - A SYMPOSIUM	
Sir Frank Harrison's Raisings	24
OVERSEAS SHOWS AND REPORTS	
ADS Convention	77
Wilkins, Peter	
RHS Early Daffodil Competition Results	83
RHS Daffodil Show Results	88

Index

Galanthus
allenii 62
Anglesey Abbey 57
Bertram Anderson 59
Blewbury Tart 79
Blonde Inge 79
caucasicus 'double' 60
caucasicus hort. 62
caucasicus var. *monostictus* 57,59
Comet 59,62
Cordelia 59
Cowhouse Green 79,106
Daglingworth 72
Ecusson d'Or 79
elwesii 57,59,60,61, 62,63
elwesii var. *monostictus* 62,63,80
Flore Pleno 59,60
Ginns' Imperati 59
gracilis 59
Greenish 57
Henry's white Lady 80
Hiemalis-Group 62
Hill Poë 60
Hippolyta 59
Jaquenetta 59
John Gray 59
Ketton 59
krasnovii 79
Lady Beatrix Stanley 60
Lady Elphinstone 79
Magnet 59
Miller's Late 62
Mrs McNamara 57
nivalis 57,59,79,80
nivalis, 'Flore Pleno' 59,60
nivalis 'Greenish' 57
nivalis 'Viridapice' 57
peshmenii 61,62
plicatus 57,59,62
plicatus subsp. *byzantinus* 80
Primrose Warburg 79
Ray Cobb 79
reginae-olgae 62
rizehensis 79
Ronald Mackenzie 72
S. Arnott 59
Sandersii 79

Sandhill Gate 80
Titania 59
Tubby Merlin 59
Viridapice 57
Washfield Warham 57
Wendy's Gold 57,79

Narcissus
Abbey Elizabeth 70
Abracadabra 75
abscissus 16,17
Accent 56
Achduart 69,77,98, 100,102
Actaea 27,28.47
Affirmation 77
Ahwahnee 101,102
Akala 76
Akepa 47
alcaracensis 15
All American 77
alpestris 16,77,94,95,96
Alpine Express 74
Alto 77
Altun Ha 86,96,101,102
Always 77
Amazing Grace 77,101
American Dream 65,77
American Heritage 65
American Shores 5
Angel Eyes 77
Angel's Whisper 75
Angelito 101
Anitra 76
Ard Righ 45
Ardress 102
Art Nouveau 77
Ashland 77
Ashmore 86
assoanus 15,73
asturiensis 18,19,46,71
asturiensis 'Wavertree' 93
Atholl Palace 87
Atlas Gold 78
Atom 71
Audrey Robinson 23
aureus 83
Auspicious 101
Badbury Rings 86,102
Bandit 69,76,96
Banstead Village 86
Barbary Gold 101

Barnesgold 76,101,102
Beaulieu 81
Beautiful Dream 102
Bebop 23
Belinensis 96
Berceuse 101
Bere Ferrers 66
Best Friend 100
bicolor 16
Blisland 21,24,87
Bobbysoxer 23
Bon Bon 25
Border Beauty 55
Boscastle 87
Boslowick 105
Bright Angel 25,27
Broadway Village 81
Brodick 86
Broomhill 76
bujei 15
bulbocodium 15,18,94,95
bulbocodium 'Mrs McConnell' 95
bulbocodium graellsii 16
bulbocodium subsp. *bulbocodium* 18,77, 99
bulbocodium subsp. *conspicuus* 95
bulbocodium subsp. *praecox* var. *paucinervis* 78
bulbocodium var. *citrinus* 83,94
bulbocodium var. *citrinus* 'Belinensis' 96
bulbocodium var. *conspicuus* 96
bulbocodium var. *obesus* 96
Burning Bush 48,86
Burntollet 102
Cairntoul 76,86
calcicola 71,96
Calleva 102
Cameo Baron 75
Cameo Prince 75
Cameo Sun 76
Camoro 106
Campion 21,23
canariensis 94
Candlepower 94

Cantabile 20,21,22,23, 24,26,28
cantabricus 16,78,94
cantabricus subsp. *cantabricus* 95
cantabricus var. *monophyllus* 78,95
Cantata 26
Canticle 24
Capax Plenus 38,41
Cape Point 86,99
Capree Elizabeth 75
Cariad 46,47
Carib Gypsy 77
Carlton 13
Carole Lombard 77,86
Castle Howard 97
Catawba 25
Catlin Jewel 26
Cavalryman 86
cazorlanus 95
× *cazorlanus* 15
Cedar Hills 86
Celestial Fire 96
Centrefold 75,76
Champeen 75
Chapel Bells 77
Chelsea Girl 97
Cherrygardens 97
Chesterton 28
China Doll 97
Chinchilla 102
Chobe River 101
Chromacolor 56
Clare 23,77
Clouded Yellow 86
Clouds Rest 5
Colley Gate 100
Colourful 102
Colville 24
Conestoga 77,86,96
Cool Crystal 87,96,97, 100,102
Cool White 77
Corbiere 81
cordubensis 83,94,95,96
Cornell 77
Coromandel 77
Cosmic Dance 77
Cotinga 56
Crevette 73
Crimson Rim 23,25

109

Crowndale 87,97,101, 102
cuatrecasasii 95
Cushendall 24
cyclamineus 18,23,47, 48,49,94,95,96
Cyclataz 94
Dactyl 25
Dailmanach 76,100
Dandubar 83
Dateline 96,101
Dawn Chorus 46
Daydream 102
Delta Queen 77
Dewy Rose 48
Dickcissel 105
Dimple 23
Dinkie 49
Doctor Hugh 86,102
Dorchester 5,75,77,87, 96,101,102
Douglasbank 94,95
Dove Wings 81
Dreamland 26
Drumlin 105
dubius 14,15,73,95,96
Dunadry Inn 101
Dunkery 102
Dunley Hall 76,102
Dylan Thomas 25
Eastbrook Sunrise 81
Ebony 76
Egmont Charm 75
Eira 106
El Camino 47
Eland 77,100
Electrus 5
Elizabeth Ann 87
Elka 83,94,95,96
Elmbridge 97
Embee 26
Emerald Sea 47
Emerald 25
Emperor 49
Empress 49
ernii 99
Ethos 101,102
Evesham 86,96,102
Explosion 77
Eyrie 77
Eystettensis 38,41
Fairy Chimes 87,97,98

Fairy Footsteps 24
Fairy Gold 95
Fairy Spell 24
Felindre 48
fernandesii 15,47,49,77, 96
fernandesii var. *major* 47
Ferndown 100
Filoli 5,101,102
Fire-Blade 97
Fireblade 102
Flash Affair 74
Fortescue 76,77
Fragrant Rose 86,102
Frank's Fancy 77
Fresh Lime 5
Gamay 56
Gay Kybo 66,87,96,97
Gipsy Queen 94
Glenfarclas 49
Goff's Caye 76
Gold Bond 75,77,86,102
Gold Convention 76,96
Golden Dawn 56
Golden Joy 76
Golden Spur 45
Golden Vale 76,81
Goldfinger 5,77,81,96, 97,100,101,102
Goldhanger 81
Graduation 65
Green Tragedy 25
Greenpark 21,24
Gull 5,76
Gweal 26
Hadlow Down 5
Haiku 23,25
Hambledon 77,96
Harbour View 77
Harmony Bells 46
Hartlebury 96
Hawera 15,48,98
Heamoor 81
hedraeanthus 15
Henry Irving 45
Hever 97
High Society 97,105
hispanicus 'Patrick Synge' 94
Holme Fen 102
Homestead 77

Honey Bells 46,49
Honeybourne 86
Honeyorange 77
Hoopoe 102,105
Hummingbird 77
Hurrah 77
Ice Chimes 48
Ice Dancer 77
Ice Wings 77,96,97,99
Impeccable 75
Inca 48,49
incurvicervicus 83
Indian Maid 77
Innishowen Head 24
intermedius 83
Intrigue 77,102
Inverpolly 86
Irish Affair 77
Irish Mist 74
Irvington 77
Isambard 81
Ita 102
Izzy's Gem 26
Jack Wood 83
Jake 5,86,100
Jetfire 95
Jodi 87
John Wall 95
jonquilla 47,49,95
jonquilla minor 15
jonquilla var. *fernandesii* 95
jonquilla var. *henriquesii* 77,83,94,95
Jumblie 53
June Lake 5,86,97,101
Kaydee 96
Killearnan 21,22,23, 25,87
King Alfred 48,49
Kingsgrove 102
Kiwi Magic 76
Kiwi Ruler 76
Korora Bay 102
Ladies Choice 87
Lady Di 75
Lady Serena 23,24
lagoi 18,19
Las Vegas 55
Lemon Drops 105
Lemon Silk 81
Lennymore 76,77

Lilac Charm 100,102
Limequilla 47,100
Limpkin 101
Lisbarnett 48
Little Gem 49
Little John Walker 94
Little Polly 87
Little Rusky 77
Littlefield 106
Lobularis Grandiplenus 38,41,42
Lobularis Plenus 38,41
Lone Star 77
Lonesome Dove 77
Lordship 74
Lorikeet 5
Lucy Jane 25
lugoi 19
Lynx 76
Lyric 23
M. J. Berkeley 45
Magician 47
Magnificence 49
Mahmoud 73
Mangaweka 75
Manly 87,105
Marjorie Treveal 96
Mary Oliver 25
Marzo 83
Matador 48
Maximus 49
Maya Angelou 25
Mereworth 96
Midget 94
Millie Galyon 48
Minicycla 94,95
Minnow 71
minor 'Douglasbank' 94
Minuet 49
Mission Bells 46
Misty Glen 88,100,102
Mite 48,94,95
Mitzy 94,95
Mizzen Head 24
Modulux 77
moleroi 16,17
Momento 102
Monal 46,49
Monticello 77
montserratii 17
Moon Shadow 76,86, 96,100

Index

moschatus 16,94
moschatus var. *alpestris* 16
Mount Fuji 102
Mowser 87
Moyle 24,26,77
Mrs McConnell 95
× *munozii-garmandiae* 16,95
Nanus Plenus 38,41,42
Nether Barr 101
nevadensis 96
New Hope 76
New Life 81
New Penny 75
Newport 77
Niantic 25
No Worries 75
Nonchalant 86,97,102
Noteworthy 77
Notre Dame 77
obvallaris 44,95
ochroleucus 83
odoratus 83
Omega 25
Oregon Beauty 46
Oregon Pioneer 65,77
Pacific Rim 97
Page Lee 77
pallidiflorus 17
Pampaluna 5
Panache 76,86
Pango 77
papyraceus 73,95
Patois 21,23
Patrick Synge 94
Pay Day 65
Peaseblossom 71
Penjerrick 24
People's Princess 75
Peppercorn 81
Pequenita 83,84
Perfeck 76
Perky 75
Petrel 100
Phalarope 75
Pheasant's Eye 28
Phebe 25
Picarillo 71
Picoblanco 83,95
Pidget 23
Pipestone 48
Pipit 105

poeticus 16,17,21,22, 23,24,26
poeticus hellenicus 24
poeticus physaloides 24
poeticus recurvus 27
poeticus var. *recurvus* 77
Poet's Way 23
Polar Morn 74
Polar Sky 76
Poppy's Choice 87
Port Noo 102
Portfolio 102
Precocious 105
Predator 81
Presidential Pink 101
pseudonarcissus 38,44
pseudonarcissus aureus 37
pseudonarcissus subsp. *eugeniae* 94,95
pseudonarcissus subsp. *pseudonarcissus* 13
Puhoi 75
Pukenui 75
pumilus 19
Purbeck 97,100,101,102
Quail 56
Quasar 47
Quetzal 25
Quick Step 45,47,48, 49,101
Quince 53
Radiant Gem 76
Rainbow 100
Rapture 75,81,97
Ravenhill 102
Red Atom 75
Red Hugh 24
Regal Bliss 102
Reggae 56
Rejoice 77
Remembered Kiss 77
Ridgecrest 96,101
Rijnveld's Early Sensation 46,49
Rikki 97
Ring Fence 77,86,97
Ringer 27
Ringleader 97,101
Ringstead 73
Rip van Winkle 38,41, 42
River Queen 101

Rockall 76,96
romieuxii 78
Rondo 26
Royal China 97,100
Royal Marine 86
Rupert Brooke 26
rupicola 11,15,16
rupicola subsp. *watieri* 11,96
Sabine Hay 49,69
Saint Budock 81
Sam Hunt 26
Samsara 77,100
Sargeant's Caye 96
Saturn Five 75
Savoir Faire 77,86,102
scaberulus 83
Sea Gift 71
Sea Green 21,23.25
Sea White 25
Segovia 77
seguriensis 15
Serena Beach 101,102
Sergeants Caye 97
Shangani 86
Sharnden 96
Sheelagh Rowan 75,86, 99,100
Sheer Joy 97
Sheilah 25
Shykoski 75
Silent Valley 86,97,105
Silken Sails 102
Silver Bells 45,46,47, 48,49
Silver Chimes 87,99
Silver Crystal 102
Silver Surf 102
Skiffle 71
Small Talk 94
Snipe 48,95,96
Snowy Morn 74,76
Snug 71
Soft Focus 86
Solar Tan 96
Soleil d'Or 94
Songket 77
Soprano 97
Sperrin Gold 5
Spindletop 77
Spring Break 77
Springston Charm 76

Springston Remembrance 75
Spun Honey 76,87
Stafford 77
Stanway 86
State Express 86
Steffi 76
Straight Arrow 48
Stratosphere 69,87, 96,97,99
Sun Disc 71
Super Seven 77
Surfside 47,83
× *susannae* 16
Swallow Wing 96
Swedish Sea 77
Taffeta 78
Tamar Double White 28
Tamar Fire 66
Tarlatan 78
Tart 25
Tasgem 87
tazetta 38,50,94
Tehidy 77
Telamonius Plenus 37, 39,40
Temple Splendour 76
Ten of Diamonds 25
The Alliance 56
Tiffany Jade 86
Tino Pai 26
Topkapi 102
Topolino 95
tortifolius 14,15
Tracey 75
Treble Chance 78
Trena 55,81
triandrus 15,16,46,77,95
triandrus concolor 15
triandrus pallidulus 15,16
triandrus subsp. *pallidulus* 16
triandrus subsp. *triandrus* 95,99
triandrus subsp. *triandrus* var. *triandrus* 46,49
triandrus var. *concolour* 94
triandrus var. *loiseleurii* 77
triandrus var. *triandrus* 100,101
Trimon 95
Tripartite 77,99

111

Triple Crown 69,86
Trumpet Warrior 75,96,
    99
Tucaman 76
Tuckahoe 77
Tuesday's Child 102
Tête-à-tete 53,83
Tweeny 71,72
Tyson's Corner 77
× *ubriquensis* 94
Ulster Bank 77
Uncle Duncan 97
Unique 87,96,105
Urbane 77
Utiku 75
Val d'Incles 96
Van Sion 19,37
Verona 100
Verran Rose 101
Vers Libre 23
Vienna Woods 25,77
viridiflorus 47
Wavertree 94
Whisky Mac 86
White Owl 48
White Star 86,98,102
White Tea 102
Wild Card 76
willkommii 95
Williamsburg 77

Xit 77,97
Xunantunich 76
Yellow Pet 78
Yellow Xit 71,77
yepesii 15
Young Blood 96,102
Ypsilante 27

Tulipa
Arabian Mystery 93
armena 34
Barbados 56
Big Smile 101
Black Hero 55
boeotica 34
Candy Club 56
Caravelle 101
Chato 55,56
City of Vancouver 30
cretica 94,95,96
doerfleri 34
Dordogne 55
dubia 34
Duc van Toll 8
ferganica 34
Flaming Parrot 55
Flashback 56
fosteriana 34
Françoise 101
Gavota 55

gesneriana 34,35
Globe 55
Golden Apeldoorn 101
Golden Melody 101
greigii 34
Havran 55
Horizon 55
humilis violacea 94
James Wild 104
kaufmanniana 34
kurdica 94
La Courtine 55
Lac van Rijn 8
lanata 34
Long Lady 101
Lord Stanley 31
Mabel 31
Maureen 68,103
Mazda 55
Menton 55,68,103
Mirella 101
Monte Carlo 30
Mrs John T Scheepers 68
Olympic Flame 93
Orange Princess 55
orphanidea 34
Ottawa 30
Pieter de Leur 101
Pink Impression 93,101
Princess Irene 55

Princesse Charmante 56
pulchella var. *coerulea-
    occulata* 94
pulchella var. *violacea* 94
Queen of Night 55
Raijka 55
Red Princess 55,56
Renown 68
Rory McEwen 103
Royal Sovereign 103
schrenkii 34
stapfii 95
sylvestris subsp. *australis*
    83
Talisman 103
The Bishop 30
tschimganica 34
tubergeniana 34
undulatifolia 34
Verona 55
Vivex 93,101
vvedenskyi 34
Wakefield 103
World Expression 55
World's Favourite 101
zenaidi 34
Zomerschoon 8

INDEX TO ADVERTISERS

American Daffodil Society, The	17
Carncairn Daffodils (Broughshane)	56
Daffodil Society, The	12
Daffodil Society of New Zealand, the National	40
Hofflands Daffodils	82
Mitsch Daffodils	92
Ringhaddy Daffodils	64
Rukšans, Jānis	58
Scamp, R. A.	19
Walkers Bulbs	10